ELECTING RECESSION

The Impact of Presidential Elections on Financial Markets and the Economy

Mark,
Enjoy the Book!
— Jason Schenker

JASON SCHENKER

Copyright © 2016 Prestige Professional Publishing, LLC

All rights reserved.

ELECTING RECESSION

*The Impact of Presidential Elections
on Financial Markets and the Economy.*

BY JASON SCHENKER

No part of this publication may be reproduced, copied, stored in or transmitted into a data retrieval system, or transmitted in any form, or by any means (electronic, mechanical, photocopying, recording, or any other method) without written permission of the publisher, Prestige Professional Publishing, LLC.

ISBN: 978-0-9849728-3-8 *Paperback*
978-0-9849728-6-9 *Ebook*

For my wife, Ashley.

CONTENTS

INTRODUCTION	7
CHAPTER 1 WHY I WROTE THIS BOOK FOR YOU	11
CHAPTER 2 HOBSON'S CHOICES FOR PARTY LOYALISTS	17
CHAPTER 3 BATTLEGROUND STATES AND POLITICAL SCHLIEFFEN PLANS	27
CHAPTER 4 ECONOMIC CONDITIONS AHEAD OF THE 2016 ELECTION	37
CHAPTER 5 FINANCIAL MARKETS AHEAD OF THE 2016 ELECTION	59
CHAPTER 6 ELECTION CYCLICALITY AND ELECTION-RECESSION WINDOWS	69
CHAPTER 7 FINANCIAL MARKETS AND PRESIDENTIAL ELECTIONS	91
CHAPTER 8 IMPORTANT CONDITIONS UNLIKELY TO CHANGE	101
CHAPTER 9 RESPONDING TO RISKS AND CHALLENGES	125
END NOTES	133
ABOUT THE AUTHOR	143
RANKINGS	145
ABOUT THE PUBLISHER	149
DISCLAIMERS	159

INTRODUCTION

WHOEVER WINS

Have you ever seen the movie *Alien versus Predator*?

It's a not-so-great movie with a really great tagline that could be applied to the coming U.S. presidential election: "Whoever wins… we lose." Don't get me wrong, there are plenty of reasons to prefer one presidential candidate over the other, but there are a number of reasons why, unfortunately, it may not matter for the economy. In the near-term, the risk of a U.S. recession is high, as data point to slowing growth. Plus, a historical trend of *election cyclicality* — when recessions and presidential elections collide — presents a historical reason to be concerned about recession.

In the medium-term, risks from the national debt, entitlements, demographics, and automation threaten the economic fabric of our country. These huge, ugly threats are nastier than anything from an *Alien* movie, but they are not even part of the debate. Yet, they will have a huge impact on the U.S. economy in the next four to eight years.

Recent Economic Data

U.S. economic data have weakened, and the odds of another U.S. recession have increased. This was a topic in my last book, *Recession-Proof*, which came out in February 2016. The near-term economic data are still not good. It's not a coincidence that this is my second book out this year with the word "recession" in the title.

Some of the biggest exposures to the U.S. economy come from a few key sectors, including heavy industry, oil & gas, and finance. Some of these risks are already front and center. But, some of the greatest risks to U.S. economic growth in the near term come from sectors people believe are doing well: retail sales and auto sales.

Election Cyclicality

In my analysis, I am most concerned with recession starts, since the United States has been in its current business cycle expansion for over seven years — since the Great Recession ended in June 2009. It's been a long cycle, and it could come to a close soon.

When targeting recession starts, I discovered a certain kind of *election cyclicality,* which has two main attributes related to how recessions and presidential elections coincide. One attribute of *election cyclicality* is the *election-recession window*, which increases the odds of a recession starting shortly before or shortly after a U.S. presidential election. This has held true for all but one recession since the Great Depression. The second attribute is tied to a *term limit on growth*, which has held true since 1854.

Election-Recession Window

As we look at the timing of recession starts, I present information about the narrow timeframe in which recession starts happen around presidential election. It's something I call the *election-recession window*.

If we look back to all of the official recessions since 1854, we find that the *election-recession window* has actually narrowed since 1928. In other words, since the Great Depression, recessions have started closer to elections than before. Plus, there has only been one recession start since 1928 that did not occur in the 11 months leading up to a presidential election, or in the 13 months after a presidential election. This is a key part of the *election-recession window* — and we are in it right now!

Term Limit on Growth

There are elections without recessions, but there have never been three consecutive presidential terms without a recession start. Never. This means that we are likely to see the next recession start before the end of Obama's second term, or during the next presidential term.

Since 1854, the historical maximum number of presidential terms without a recession start is two. There have been no exceptions. Think of it as a *term limit on growth*, which is the second attribute of *election cyclicality*. I go into full detail on the subject of *election cyclicality,* and the impact of U.S. presidential elections on U.S. economic data, in Chapter 6.

Long-Term Risks

As we look further into the future, there are bigger, major, long-term risks to the economy. These include the U.S. national debt, entitlement expenditures, demographics, and automation risks to the labor force.

The good news is that some of these risks could be mitigated, if they were addressed. The bad news is that these risks have been largely avoided during the current election cycle. This means that the next president is unlikely to address these risks, which threaten the American economy on an existential level. In fact, no matter who the next president is, they are very likely to make these bigger, scarier things worse for the American economy.

These risks are big trains coming down the tracks towards a ravine without a bridge. Neither candidate is likely to build the bridge required. So, it's up to you to prepare yourself!

I have dedicated Chapter 9 to helping you respond to these risks and challenges ahead.

CHAPTER 1

WHY I WROTE THIS BOOK FOR YOU

I wrote this book to help you prepare for the potential impact of the coming U.S. election. U.S. presidential elections are important for the economy and financial markets, which is why they get a lot of coverage in business media — and why there is often significant market commentary about elections written by financial analysts.

People talk about how the different candidates could impact the economy or financial markets, but such talk is often informed by political positions individuals hold, rather than an objective analysis of the data. When discussing the potential financial market and economic impact of the coming U.S. election with others, I observed that people's sentiments about the economic impact of presidential candidates were often more visceral and emotional, rather than based on an analysis of any kind of data.

It's one thing to talk about data and to have a feeling about a candidate, but it is a very different thing to actually look at the historical data objectively to identify trends. That's also a little bit more difficult, and it's something that's been done infrequently — and often with a political bent.

I have tried very hard in this book to present numbers as they are, not how I (or anyone else) would like them to be.

Objectivity, Correlation, and Causality
When I started working on this book, my mind was a complete blank slate in terms of expectations. What you'll read in this book about the results of my analysis was a surprise to me, and it might be a surprise for you, too.

Before I had written a word of this book, I knew two things. First, I knew that this kind of analysis had not been performed in this way before. Second, I knew that the data was going to show something cool. I wasn't sure what I was going to find, but I was pretty sure it would be interesting.

I have a Master's in Economics and I've been a professional business economist since 2004. I've looked at a lot of data over the years — data about the economy, commodity markets, foreign exchange rates, interest rates, the oil and gas industry, the metals industry, automotive parts & vehicle manufacturing, and material handling. I see a lot of new data all the time, and the one thing I can tell you is that every time I see new data, there are surprises.

Sometimes the data shows you what you expect, but other times the data shows you something wild. My analysis of historical recession data was a mix of mild and wild, as you will see.

Implications extrapolated from data can be very important — and they can impact you personally. In the chapters ahead, I present the potential near-term and medium-term economic and financial market implications of the 2016 U.S. presidential election.

No Assumptions
I'm not Glenn Beck or Ann Coulter or James Carville. I'm not a political pundit, and I don't have an axe to grind in this book against one party or the other. This isn't to say that I do not have biases. Of course, I do. But when I wrote this book, I did the analysis first.

Correlation and Causation
I have tried to share my analysis in this book as objectively as possible. In a recent presentation I gave, I shared my analysis showing that unemployment rates had fallen for every Democratic president since the end of World War II except Carter, and that unemployment rates had risen for every Republican president except Reagan. One executive quickly jumped in: "Republican unemployment rates rise because Republican presidents follow Democrats, and Democrat rates fall, because they follow Republicans!" While this is not a completely accurate representation of presidential term sequence, it does underscore a very important issue: the correlation of historical data are not necessarily indicative of causality. I will talk about this more when I get to the topic of unemployment and other U.S. economic data in Chapter 5.

This Time It's Different

I don't expect the business cycle to be different this time around; I expect historical *election cyclicality* will hold. However, I do believe that this book — and its analysis — is different.

When people think about the financial impact of elections, there is a tendency for analysts on Wall Street and observers on Main Street to focus almost exclusively on equity markets. This book is different, because it takes a look at equity markets *and* economic indicators, currency rates, oil prices, and precious metals prices. Of course, as you will see, some data and markets can be greatly influenced by the outcome of presidential elections, while others have trended independently. The ramifications of presidential elections for the economy and financial markets have not been looked at previously in such an intercorrelated market framework.

I find this kind of cross-market approach to be very helpful in my regular market forecasting, as the President and Chief Economist of Prestige Economics. It's worked out well so far, and Bloomberg News has ranked me a top forecaster in 31 different categories for my forecast accuracy since 2011. These rankings have been awarded for my accuracy in predicting economic indicators, foreign exchange rates, energy prices, metals prices, and agricultural prices. Looking beyond equity markets produces some unique, high-value insights that someone could otherwise miss.

Based on my analysis, U.S. presidential elections may actually be more important than previously expected for the economy. It's important to look at how U.S. economic indicators, like unemployment, industrial production, and GDP growth respond to different parties holding the reigns of power, as well as to presidential elections in general.

Be Prepared, Whoever Wins
This book provides an objective look at recent U.S. presidential elections and presidencies, to glean from them some insights into what the outcome of the 2016 presidential election might hold for the economy and financial markets. Equally important, however is the question: What is unlikely to change no matter which candidate is elected?

Whether we end up with Hillary Clinton or Donald Trump, I want you to be prepared for the potential outcomes — based on the numbers. You may not be happy with the outcome in terms of who you want to see elected president, but maybe you can be prepared. Some things are unlikely to differ much, regardless of the candidate and party of the next president. Some of those things are good, but some of them are bad.

CHAPTER 2

HOBSON'S CHOICES FOR PARTY LOYALISTS

This is not a book about the history of American politics, but I have included this chapter to help set the stage for our discussion. After all, even before we dig into the current economic situation or the intersection of politics and economics, I need to share a brief overview of the historical and current political dynamics in the United States. For U.S. political aficionados, this section is likely to seem somewhat rudimentary, but this information will help outline the political landscape and battlefield ahead of the 2016 presidential election. I think this is an important section because, especially for foreign readers, or those who do not happen to be deeply steeped in politics, this should provide some fundamental background information.

Two Party Winner Takes All
The political system in the United States is a winner-take-all voting system that favors two parties. There are other parties, but there are only two political parties that have a shot at winning the presidency in 2016: Republicans and Democrats. The dominating parties have changed over time, but these are the main two now.

Of course, there are other parties beyond these two major parties. According to ballotpedia.org, there are 30 other political parties participating in the 2016 presidential election, as of April 2016. Three of these minor parties are recognized in more than 10 states: the Libertarian Party (33 states), the Green Party (21 states), and the Constitution Party (13 states).[1] There may be a lot of parties, but because of the winner-take-all nature of the U.S. voting system, the final presidential contest comes down to an election between these two main party candidates.

The *de facto* two-party system has generally been the reality since the election of 1796, which followed George Washington's unanimous elections in 1789 and 1792. In other words, other than for the election of the first President of the United States, most elections have been between two main parties.[2] There have been third parties at times, but the winner-take-all system favors consolidation to two parties. Of course the nature of the two main U.S. political parties — Republican and Democrats — has evolved and changed over time, as have their platforms, voter bases, and core values on critical issues like slavery, abolition, civil rights, and isolationism. The parties have changed much over time, but the number of main parties has not. For most of American history, there have been two main players. That's a product of winner-take-all voting.

The Democratic party traces its lineage back to Thomas Jefferson, which gets very confusing, because he was actually a member of something called the Democratic-Republican party. What's in a name? In this case a lot of confusion.

If we look for presidents that identified as Democrats, Andrew Jackson was the first modern Democratic president. He was first elected president in 1828.[3] The first Republican president was Abraham Lincoln, who was first elected president in 1860.

Primaries and Caucuses
In their modern incarnations, U.S. political parties push a nominated candidate forward in the race to the White House through a funneling process that involves primaries and caucuses, in which the parties each elect a nominee ahead of the general election.

Everyone wants to be President. It seems, at least, like every politician does!

Ahead of the 2016 election, there were initially 17 main Republican candidates — so many, in fact, that for a number of the debates between the candidates there had to be two separate stages, with the lower polling candidates debating before the higher polling candidates. As for the Democrats, there were five main candidates registered, but only two won delegates, Bernie Sanders and Hillary Clinton. In order to narrow down which politician becomes his or her party champion, the party members must have an election before the election. The culmination of this process occurs at party conventions.

Conventions, Primaries, and Caucuses

There are two ways that voters in the two main political parties decide which candidate will be the nominee for president. They vote in primaries and caucuses, in which the candidates collect delegates, which are awarded based on victories in those primaries and caucuses. There are also superdelegates in each party, who are party insiders whose votes are not tied to any specific primary or caucus outcome.

Once the primaries and caucuses have been concluded in all 50 states, Washington D.C., and U.S. territories, the parties hold conventions at which they nominate one candidate for president. For the Democrats, the nomination of Hillary Clinton was confirmed at the Democratic party convention in Philadelphia between 25 and 28 July 2016. For the Republicans, the nomination of Donald Trump was confirmed at the Republican party convention in Cleveland between 18 and 21 July 2016.

One major downside of the primary and caucus system, is that it can create internal party strife and conflict. It can also provide ammunition for the opposing party's candidate during the general election.

Ahead of the 2016 election, both parties found themselves dealing with internal challenges to the candidates they would ultimately nominate for President. The Republican party had a very contentious primary season and found itself quite divided, as Donald Trump, a political outsider with a large personality clinched the nomination. Republicans going into this election now find themselves with a Hobson's choice.

Hobson's Choice

Let's talk about a Hobson's Choice for a minute. Maybe you've heard this phrase before. Well, let's make it a bit more tangible. This is a portrait of Thomas Hobson. Maybe you'd rather see a picture of Hillary or Trump, but this is, quite literally, your Hobson's choice.

Hobson was a stable master in sixteenth century England. He ran his stables in such a way that when you wanted a horse from him, you were offered whatever horse was in the first stable. You could refuse that horse, but then you wouldn't get one at all.

There are difficult decisions that people make, and a Hobson's choice is one of them. This image comes from the National Gallery, in London, where it used to hang.[4] It wasn't hanging there in June 2016. There were paintings of Kate Middleton and The Spice Girls instead.

Ahead of the 2016 party conventions, the primaries and caucuses were hard fought by both parties, and there were expectations of potentially contested conventions for both the Democrats and the Republicans. Traditional Republicans threatened to contest a Trump nomination on the Republican side, while Sanders supporters threatened to contest a Clinton nomination on the Democrats' side. Neither contest happened with any level of success.

Hillary is the Hobson's Choice For Democrats
For the Democrats, the primary season involved a smaller field of candidates, but the interjection of Bernie Sanders, and his surprising success, shifted some of the political dynamics and discourse of the Democratic party. There were a number of Bernie supporters who were pushing a "Bernie or Bust" motto ahead of the Democratic convention in Philadelphia. But, much like potentially displeased Republican voters who did not support Trump, Bernie supporters have a Hobson's choice to make. They can either support Hillary or not. Bernie was such an important part of the Democratic party primary season that it was critical for the party that he endorse Hillary at the Democratic convention, which he did.

The Hobson's choice for Democrats is Hillary Clinton. She's it.

Trump is the Hobson's Choice For Republicans
For Republicans the choice is Trump. No matter how many traditional Republican politicians and voters may have opposed Trump's candidacy, they have a Hobson's choice now, too. Trump is their horse, take him or leave him. You could either take that horse out of the stable and ride him to the White House, or leave him where he stands. One caveat on Trump: some speculated that he would potentially run as an Independent if he didn't win the Republican primary. But the truth is that probably wasn't ever going to happen. Running as an Independent is a costly — and usually futile — endeavor.

In the end, most party loyalists will take the horse they're offered. However, one senior executive I know, who's been a life-long Republican, told me, "I'll take no horse, rather than the one closest to the door, throw Mr. Hobson the finger as I walk down the road without a horse!" Poor Mr. Hobson.

The Peter Principle
Some of you reading this book may be disappointed with the presidential nominees from the two main parties. After all, a large block from each party voted for candidates who did not clinch the nomination. In fact, according to the New York Times, "only 9 percent of America chose Trump and Clinton as the nominees."[5]

I often hear people say, "How did this happen?" I think the Peter Principle goes a long way to answering that question.

The Peter Principle by Laurence J. Peter and Raymond Hull is a book focused on how people reach their level of ineffectiveness, and dedicates a full chapter to politics. Peter and Hull noted in their research that, all governments and political systems are "characterized by the same accumulation of redundant and incompetent personnel."[6] For this reason, "any government, whether it is a democracy, a dictatorship, a communistic or free enterprise bureaucracy, will fall when its hierarchy reaches an intolerable state of maturity."[7] In other words, incompetency increases within the ranks of governments and political structures over time. That's a very bad thing!

I often hear people, even if they are party loyalists, say that they seem to be dissatisfied with their choices. They may make the Hobson's choice, and they may ride that horse to the election, but they may not be happy about it. They'll take it, but they wish they had another option.

If you happen to be a dissatisfied member of a party that is not completely content with your party's nominee for president, there are other parties for whom they can vote, including the list of parties mentioned earlier. Those of you who accept the Hobson's choice and vote for your party, may wonder, as a student of Peter and Hull once did, if "the world is run by smart men who are...putting us on, or by imbeciles who really mean it."[8]

I think they mean it, but I could be wrong.

Voting From The Holy Roman Empire
After the Democratic and Republican party conventions, candidates begin to focus on the coming presidential election. Presidents capture the White House, however, not by winning total popular votes, but by amassing electoral votes. Like in the Holy Roman Empire, electors chose the leader. The group of U.S. electors is called the electoral college, and they are apportioned to the states and Washington D.C. in a similar manner as the Congressional power of each state.

Each state receives one electoral vote for each Congressman and Senator from that state. Plus, three additional electoral votes are allocated to Washington D.C., making the total number of electors 538 (100 senators, 435 congressmen, and 3 D.C. electors).[9]

The democratic part of this process kicks in when the electors usually (but are not required to) cast their votes for the presidential candidate that wins their state — or district, in the case of Washington D.C. Usually these votes are allocated as winner take all, but there are exceptions.

There are a few different reasons why the system works this way, and both of these reasons harken back to the founding of the original 13 United States. The structure of the elector system was designed to prevent the direct election of a president by the people, as a safeguard against populists. Plus, the allocation of electoral votes was structured to balance the concerns of smaller states against the will of larger states, which also explains our bicameral allocation of votes mirrored by the electoral college.

Election Background Review

Let's review a few important takeaways from this chapter.

U.S. politics has historically been dominated by two parties, because of the U.S. winner-take-all system of voting. The two current dominant parties are the Democrats and the Republicans. Each of the two main political parties goes through its own independent voting process, using primaries and caucuses, to nominate a candidate to represent the party in the run for the U.S. presidency.

Party loyalists have a Hobson's choice when it comes to the candidate that gets the nomination. There is only one candidate per party that gets a nomination for the presidential election.

The U.S. president is chosen by electors, not by a directly democratic election process. The electors are apportioned in similar lines to congressional representation for each of the states. Electors may, but are not required to, vote for the presidential candidate who wins their state. The District of Colombia also gets three electors, although it is not a state.

Now that we've gone over some of the basics, let's talk about battleground states!

CHAPTER 3

BATTLEGROUND STATES AND POLITICAL SCHLIEFFEN PLANS

Presidential candidates have to win electoral votes in the general election that are apportioned by state, rather than by the overall popular vote. As such, they focus on the states that can get them the biggest bang for the buck. Some states have a history of consistently and reliably voting for one candidate or the other, and they get less attention during the campaigning season. The biggest attention goes to the states that could potentially land in either camp. These states are called swing states — or battleground states.

In U.S. presidential elections, the candidates have detailed plans to win the electoral votes in battleground states. The two most important fronts are Ohio and Florida.

Because of modern historical voting patterns, the chessboard of a presidential election in the United States is set well in advance. And it hinges very much on the outcome of the swing states. The parties have to craft something like a political Schlieffen Plan to win the election.

Schlieffen Plan

The Schlieffen Plan was a strategic military plan put together by the head of the German Imperial General Staff ahead of the First World War, designed to win a war quickly on two fronts against both the French and the Russians. This plan included marching orders for the German army to defeat France quickly by going through Belgium, which would be followed by a quick transfer of troops to the Eastern Front to battle the Russian army.[1]

I use the analogy of political Schieffen Plans when talking about U.S. presidential campaigns, because it highlights the planning involved and the need for candidates to win battles on multiple fronts, in order to be victorious. Yet, the greatest strength of the actual Schlieffen Plan, was also its greatest weakness. It was well planned, but it did not leave room for changes. This is also a risk for U.S. presidential campaigns, which need to focus their efforts on battleground states, but also need to have the flexibility to deploy resources to secure states that may come to be at risk.

Focus on Battleground States

Ahead of each presidential election, we should expect to see a laser-like focus by the Republican and Democratic candidates as they implement well laid-out plans to capture battleground states. These political Schlieffen Plans determine how candidates spend their money and time — where they're going to buy the most television ads, and where they will do the most handshaking, baby kissing, etc. The outcome of the election hinges on pulling these battleground states into their own camps. It's winner take all at the state level — and some states are critical.

Historical Relevance

The outcome of the U.S. presidential election depends very much on the electoral votes of battleground states. The total number of electoral votes needed to win the presidential election is 270, and although the Democrats have more votes firmly in their camp at the beginning of the campaigning season, they still need to win some swing states.

In U.S. presidential elections, the two states that every political campaign has to fight for are Ohio and Florida. Yes, there are other swing states, but they have proven less critical for determining the outcome of U.S. presidential elections. Plus, with the current exception of Pennsylvania, they also have fewer electoral votes.

Figure 3-1: Battleground State Electoral Votes in August 2016[2]

Battleground States and Electoral Votes as of 10 August 2016	
Florida	29
Pennsylvania	20
Ohio	18
Georgia	16
North Carolina	15
Virginia	13
Wisconsin	10
Colorado	9
Nevada	6
Iowa	6
Arizona	5
New Hampshire	4

Source: 270toWin

Battleground States in 2012

Based on polls ahead of the 2012 presidential election, the Republican candidate, Mitt Romney, needed to win a preponderance of the eight battleground states that were up in the air. These states (white and dotted in Figure 3-2) included New Hampshire, Virginia, Ohio, Wisconsin, Florida, Colorado, Iowa, and Nevada. To win, Romney needed to win four of these eight states — and one of those four needed to be Ohio or Florida. For Obama, the threshold to victory was much lower, based on the states that were already firmly in the Democratic camp. Obama needed to win as few as two of eight battleground states. Since all of the battleground states were within the margins of error, and the Republican requirements were much higher, a Romney win appeared much more difficult to achieve, statistically speaking.

Figure 3-2: Presidential State Polls in October 2012[3]

Just as in 2012, whoever wins the battleground states in 2016, is likely to win the election.

A Tough Tale in Texas

Ahead of the 2012 election, I had forecasted an Obama victory and reelection. As an economist based in Texas, this was a very challenging forecast to present to public audiences and clients. After all, the last time Texas voted for a Democrat to be president was in 1976.

Based on regional voting history, it was important for me to share the numbers around the battleground states, and the probabilities of the outcomes, with my clients. The polls and the statistical probabilities, however, were clear: Obama needed a smaller number of swing states to win. In Figure 3-3, you can see what the expected electoral vote count looked like ahead of the 2012 election. Obama had a firm lead in terms of expected and likely electoral votes.

Figure 3-3: Expected Electoral Votes in October 2012[4]

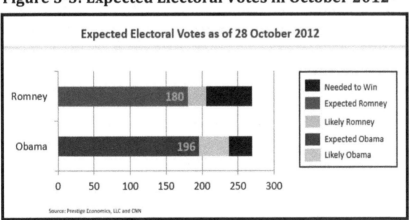

The Most Critical Battleground States: Ohio and Florida[5]

Let me take a step back here to put things in perspective. The two most important battleground states are Ohio and Florida. They have high levels of electoral votes, and they have been critical for determining the outcome of many U.S. presidential elections. They have been, however, more critical to ensure a Republican victory than for a Democratic victory.

1.) For Democrats, Ohio is critical. The last Democrat to be voted into office without winning Ohio was JFK in 1960.

2.) For Republicans, Ohio is even more critical. The last time a Republican won the presidential election without winning Ohio was... never. That's right. There have been exactly zero times that a Republican has become president without winning Ohio. The first Republican victory in Ohio dates back to 1860 with Abraham Lincoln, and the importance of Ohio is likely to remain high for the foreseeable future.

3.) For Republicans, Florida is critical, although it is somewhat less important for Democrats. The last Republican to win the White House without winning Florida was Calvin Coolidge in 1924.

If a candidate wants to be president, they must win battleground states. Both Democratic and Republican political Schlieffen Plans focus very much on Florida and Ohio, as states where a lot of advertising budget — and facetime — needs to be spent.

The Importance of Vice Presidential Candidates
Because of the importance of battleground states, the selection of a running mate for Vice President is critical — especially if that candidate can assist in capturing a battleground state (or more). Both presidential candidates have made VP choices that are designed to improve their 2016 electoral positions in battleground states.

For Hillary Clinton, the choice of Senator Tim Kaine of Virginia, should help to bring Virginia into the Democratic camp. It was a critical battleground state in 2012, and Obama eventually carried it. Hillary's selection could help keep Virginia in the Democratic camp during the 2016 presidential election. If Hillary can start off with an even bigger lead of firm Democrat-leaning states, it increases her potential to win.

For Donald Trump, the choice of Mike Pence, the governor of Indiana, should help keep Indiana in the Republican camp. Mitt Romney carried Indiana in 2012, and Pence is likely to keep it in the Republican camp. Pence also helps round out Trump's conservative appeal in the Midwest, where there are several critical battleground states.

Who's Going to Win?
At the time this book was written, it is still too early to call. But, in light of some of the topics presented in this chapter, I think that we can take an educated look at where the candidates have the greatest edge.

The Case for Hillary

Since battleground states and base mobilization will be critical in 2016, Hillary Clinton starts with an advantage on both counts. After all, the states that are firmly in the Democratic camp have more electoral votes than the states that are firmly in the Republican camp. Plus, Hillary is the wife of one of the most popular presidents in recent U.S. history — and she has the support of Obama, the current president. She is not an incumbent, but she has as much of an incumbent-like advantage, as a non-incumbent candidate probably could have. If the economy remains strong through the election, Hillary's economic narrative, as part of a post-Great Recession administration, could also be compelling.

The Case for Trump

Trump starts off behind the eight-ball, because there are more battleground states that he will need to win to be elected president. Plus, he is a Republican party outsider, which could hinder mobilization of the Republican base.

The biggest thing Trump has going for him is that presidential elections have become increasingly like reality television. This is why I was not surprised by Donald Trump's success in clinching the Republican presidential nomination. After all, more Americans voted for American Idol in 2012 than in the U.S. presidential election[6] — and Trump is a reality TV star!

Election Background Review

Let's review a few important takeaways from this chapter.

The geographic chessboard of electoral votes is already set well ahead of the election, with battleground swing states holding critical sway over the outcome of the presidential election. Democrats and Republicans approach U.S. presidential elections with political Schlieffen Plans that prioritize winning battleground states, with a focus on Florida and Ohio.

No republican has ever won the presidency without winning Ohio, and the last time a Republican won the presidency without winning Florida was in 1924. JFK was the last Democrat to win the presidential election without winning Ohio — in 1960.

Hillary Clinton is one of the most politically-connected candidates in history. Given her husband's role as a former president, she is at least as connected as John Quincy Adams, George W. Bush, and RFK. Hillary's party has an electoral vote advantage at the start, and her base is likely to be highly mobilized.

Donald Trump is the most famous presidential candidate since Ronald Reagan. He surprised many political pundits by clinching the Republican nomination, but his role as a reality television star has given him the visibility and background to be successful in the election cycle. As the general election political Schlieffen Plans focus on battleground states, mobilizing the Republican base will be critical for Trump to clinch the White House.

CHAPTER 4

ECONOMIC CONDITIONS AHEAD OF THE 2016 ELECTION

Now that we've reviewed the U.S. political landscape ahead of the 2016 presidential election, let's get to the good stuff: a discussion about the economy. The right place to begin here is by looking at current economic conditions ahead of the election. First, we will examine relevant domestic data, and then we will take a quick look at some important international economic data.

There are a number of different U.S. data series that I will present in this chapter to show the current level of U.S. economic growth and activity. In Chapter 6, I will analyze how presidential elections have historically impacted some of these data.

Domestic Data and Fed Policy
Domestically, it's good to think of the most important economic data as growth, unemployment, and inflation. These data are important, because they directly influence the policy of the Federal Reserve, also known as the Fed, which is the central bank of the United States.

Fed policy is critical for financial markets as well as the economy, so these are the three most important economic data series overall.

Critical Indicators For Markets

In addition to the big three economic data series, I have also included an analysis of other data that I find extremely valuable. These data include industrial production, the ISM Manufacturing Index, housing starts, and auto sales.

I pay close attention to industrial production and the ISM Manufacturing Index, because these two data series are highly correlated with U.S. growth. This means that in some respects industrial production and the ISM Manufacturing Index are leading economic indicators. They should help us see a bit more into what the future holds for the U.S. economy.

I will also briefly discuss the Fed Funds Rate in this chapter, although the secular move lower in rates has less to do with any kind of *election cyclicality*, and more to do with a concerted effort by recent Fed Chairmen to tame inflation.

In Chapter 6, I will present an analysis of how past Presidential election outcomes, as well as the terms and tenures of presidents, have influenced some of these economic data. I will also present some implications for the data, based on the potential outcomes of the 2016 election.

As I mentioned back in Chapter 1, causation and correlation are two different things. I have only analyzed historical economic data in the context of presidential election outcomes, presidential terms, and presidential tenures. Generally, other external economic factors have not been included in my analysis.

FRED Graphs and Recession Bars[1]
Most of the graphs in this chapter come from the Federal Reserve Economic Database (FRED). FRED graphs are free and easily accessible online at https://fred.stlouisfed.org/

A critical beneficial attribute of FRED graphs is that they include vertical gray bars to indicate the timing of past recessions, as defined by the National Bureau of Economic Research (NBER). In Chapter 6, I will talk more about recession, the various definitions thereof, and what this presidential election means for the risk of recession.

Gross Domestic Product (GDP)

GDP is a measure of economic activity within the borders of a country. It has four main parts, including Consumption (C), Government Spending (G), Investment (I), and Net Exports (NX). For those of you who like economic equations, GDP looks like this:

$$GDP = C+G+I+NX$$

Nominal and Real GDP

GDP can be presented in nominal or real terms. Nominal GDP is U.S. growth presented in current dollars, but it is not usually used for growth comparisons over time, because it is subject to inflation. Since inflation makes prices rise over time, nominal GDP growth is almost always positive, as it has been even during every recession since 1958, except the Great Recession (Figure 4-1).

Figure 4-1: U.S. Nominal GDP (Year-over-Year Rate)[2]

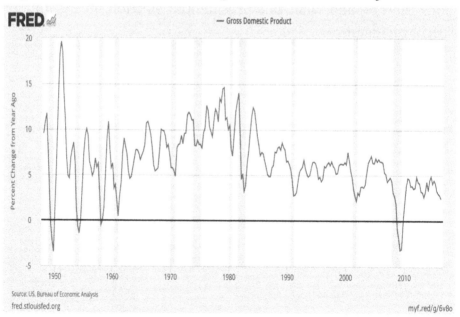

Real GDP strips out the effects of inflation, and is the dominant measure of GDP that economists and professionals use to discuss economic growth.

For Q2 2016, Real GDP was +1.2 percent quarter-over-quarter. It was the third consecutive weak report, and investment also contracted for a third quarter. On a year-over-year basis, Real GDP growth was up +1.2 percent. Real GDP growth has generally been modest since the Great Recession, with yearly growth rates between +1.6 and +2.6 percent every year since 2010.

As you can see in Figure 4-2, Real GDP growth rates during the expansionary period of the current business cycle have been at consistently lower rates than in most previous business cycles.

Figure 4-2: U.S. Real GDP (Year-over-Year Rate)[3]

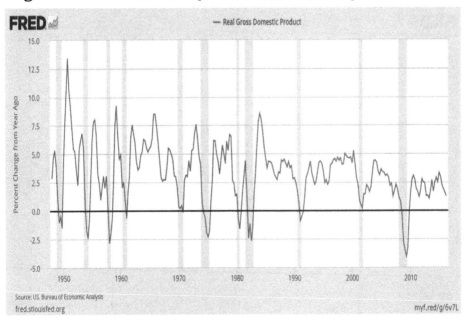

Unemployment

The unemployment rate is one measure of labor market health. It is also a cornerstone of one of the Fed's two dual mandates, full employment. Inflation is the second of the Fed's dual mandates.

The U.S. unemployment rate has fallen sharply since it peaked at 10.0 percent in October 2009, in the wake of the Great Recession. The current level of unemployment in the United States is 4.9 percent, which has been pushed lower by a mix of job creation and a drop in labor force participation rates. I will spend more time talking about labor force participation rates in Chapter 8. Basically, some people stop working or looking for work, and they drop out of the labor force. This can also send the unemployment rate lower, but it is a sign of an unhealthy labor market.

Figure 4-3: U.S. Unemployment Rate[4]

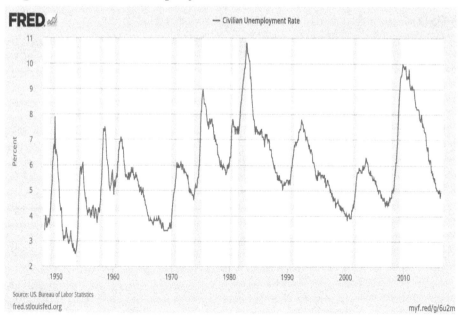

Consumer Inflation

U.S. inflation has been relatively modest in recent months. As of July 2016, total consumer inflation, as measured by the consumer price index (CPI), was up only +0.9 percent year over year, on a seasonally-adjusted basis. As you can see in the graph below, this is near a historically low level of inflation. More importantly, the Fed has a medium-term target of +2.0 percent inflation, and the current pace of total CPI is well below that level.

There is a second series of CPI that the Fed also watches called "Core" CPI, which excludes food and energy prices. That series was up +2.2 percent year over year in July 2016, which is somewhat above the Fed's +2.0 percent target.

Figure 4-4: U.S. Consumer Price Index[5]

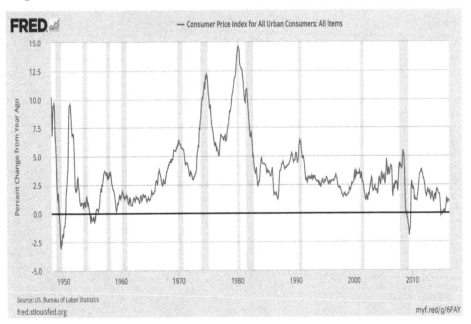

Industrial Production

Industrial production is a measure of industrial activity in factories, mining companies, and utilities. U.S. industrial production data through July 2016 conveyed an ongoing U.S. industrial and manufacturing recession with a long trend of negative year-over-year rates, only seen historically during recessions.

Since the Fed started collecting industrial production data in 1919, it has only been during recessions (or immediately after recessions) that industrial production data have been negative year-over-year for more than four consecutive months. As of July 2016, industrial production has been negative year-over-year for 11 consecutive months – much longer than the four month trend historically seen for non-recessionary periods since 1919.

Figure 4-5: U.S. Industrial Production Index[6]

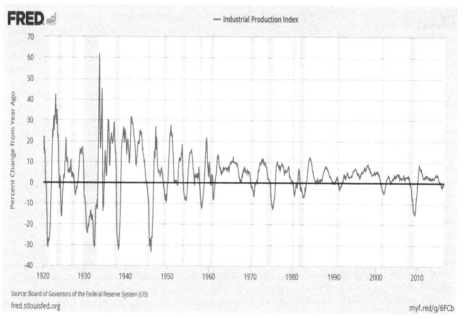

ISM Manufacturing Index

The ISM Manufacturing Index is a measure of U.S. manufacturing activity, based on survey responses gathered from purchasing managers at manufacturing companies. The breakeven level for this purchasing manager index is 50, and readings of the index below 50 are indicative of a month-over-month contraction in manufacturing activity. Multiple consecutive months of ISM readings below 50 are often leading indicators of a recession.

Through February 2016, there had been five consecutive monthly contractions in the ISM Manufacturing Index, although manufacturing activity expanded in March 2016, showing expansionary monthly activity through July 2016.

Figure 4-6: ISM Manufacturing Index[7]

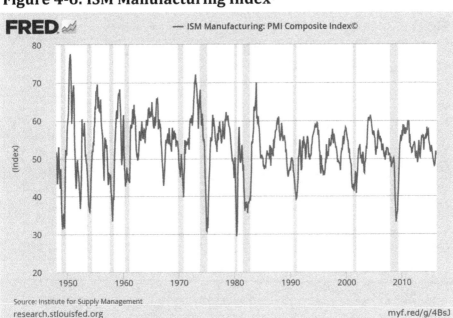

Auto Sales

The year-over-year growth in retail sales excluding autos was weaker in 2015 than in 2001 and 2008; only auto sales were strong in 2015 at 17.4 million units, versus 16.4 million in 2014. As such, if the number of light vehicles sold in 2016 falls, this would likely weigh on retail sales and the pace of consumption, contributing to slower overall U.S. GDP growth. With tightening credit, subprime auto loan issuances are likely to slow — as are auto sales. Large returning lease fleets are also likely to weigh on 2016 and 2017 new auto sales. I expect light vehicle sales in 2016 will be 16.9 million, which is 500,000 fewer vehicles than the 17.4 million vehicles in 2015. The June 2016 seasonally adjusted annual rate of light vehicle sales was only 16.7 million.

Figure 4-7: U.S. Light Vehicle Sales[8]

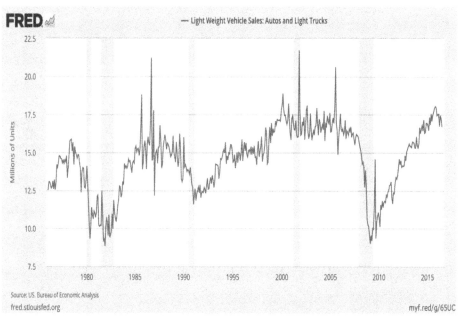

Housing Starts

Even though total U.S. housing starts have recovered since troughs seen at the end of the Great Recession, they remain low by historical standards. In fact, the current level of housing starts is at a level that has been consistent with all of the economic recessions since the 1950s — except for the 2001 recession. Housing starts remain low cyclically, because housing starts were pulled forward during the subprime boom and they have not yet recovered.

JuLY 2016 housing starts were at 1.211 million on a seasonally adjusted annual rate.

Figure 4-8: U.S. Housing Starts (SAAR)[9]

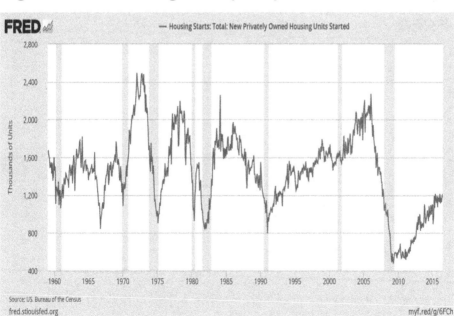

Fed Policy

Fed Funds Rates are the main policy tool of the Federal Reserve (the Fed), which is the central bank of the United States. The effective Fed Funds Rate is the interest rate at which depository institutions lend reserve balances to each other overnight.

The Fed Funds Rate is one of the main monetary policy tools that the Fed uses as a means to curb inflation — and to stimulate growth. In the 1980s, Fed Funds Rates were used to tame high inflation. More recently, with low inflation and slow growth, the Fed has left rates near historically low levels.

Higher Fed Funds Rates trap liquidity and slow inflationary pressures. However, they can also slow growth. The current Fed Funds Rate is near historically low levels, since growth rates and inflation are low.

Figure 4-9: Effective Federal Funds Rate[10]

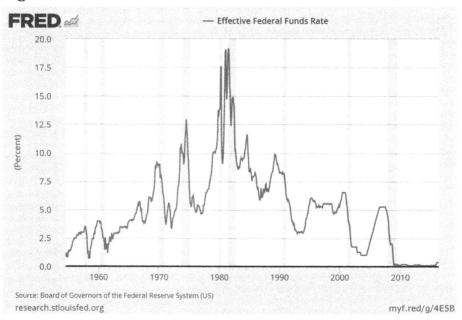

Overall U.S. Economic Conditions
By the end of 2016, I expect a U.S. recession is likely to start due to restricted access to credit, a continued recession of investment, credit risks in oil and gas, slowing U.S. auto sales, and a relatively strong greenback.

Credit Risks
Downside risks for oil and gas credit pose significant risks to financials and credit in the overall U.S. economy. This was part of a major warning issued by the Fed, FDIC, and OCC on 5 November 2015, as part of the Shared National Credit (SNC) review titled "Shared National Credits Review Notes High Credit Risk and Weaknesses Related to Leveraged Lending and Oil and Gas."[11] Although oil price risks were noted as high in the SNC, the closing price of WTI crude oil on 5 November was still $45.20. The implication of this SNC was that oil prices near or below these levels pose investment, credit, and banking risks. Oil prices subsequently fell, such that the price on 5 November of $45.20 was 34 percent higher than the average price of WTI crude oil in Q1 2016. Although oil prices rose through Q2 2016, as a result of strong driving season demand, they fell sharply in July 2016 when the summer driving season ended on the floor of the NYMEX on 20 July 2016, with the close of the August WTI crude oil contract.

Following the dismal SNC in November 2015, the Fed, FDIC, and OCC issued another Shared National Credit review on 29 July 2016.[12] It was also the first semi-annual SNC. The SNC was previously an annual review, but regulators are clearly concerned, so the new modus operandi will be a semi-annual SNC review.

The regulators are watching closely — because they have to. As noted in their own words in the title of the July SNC press release, "Risk Remains High." The July SNC review noted the same risks as the November 2015 review: leveraged lending and oil and gas.

The July 2016 SNC report also noted that oil and gas "borrower defaults and bankruptcy filings... [are] expected to continue through 2016."[13] In other words, more oil and gas company defaults and bankruptcies are coming. The recent decline in oil prices, if sustained, adds downside risks for these companies — and the economy as a whole. Banks may be exposed to the lowest risk of loss, but losses could still result in tougher lending standards in other sectors. I believe this will likely contribute to a slowing of U.S. growth.

Consumption, Credit, and Autos

Subprime auto loans helped fuel auto sales in recent years, but more credit vigilance could slow sales. As I noted previously, auto sales were the economic linchpin of consumption growth in 2015. The year-over-year growth in retail sales excluding autos was weaker in 2015 than in 2001 and 2008; only auto sales were strong in 2015 at 17.4 million units, compared to 16.4 million in 2014. As such, if the number of light vehicles sold in 2016 falls, this would likely weigh on retail sales and the pace of consumption, contributing to slower overall U.S. GDP growth. And I expect auto sales will slow as credit tightens and large returning lease fleets crowd out new light vehicle sales. The automotive aftermarket, however, is likely to be in for a solid 18 to 24 months, as vehicle owners seek to extend vehicle life during a downturn.

U.S. Economic Summary

U.S. economic data show softness in a number of critical areas going into the 2016 U.S. presidential election. Here is a review of some of the most critical data:

- **Real GDP growth** has been slow in the past three quarters, but it remains positive.
- **Nominal GDP growth** is positive, but just above levels typically seen during recessions.
- **U.S. investment** (as a component of GDP) is in a recession; it has contracted for three consecutive quarters.
- **Industrial production** is in a recession, with a trend of negative year-over-year growth rates that have historically only been seen during recessions.
- **ISM Manufacturing Index** contracted in late 2015 and early 2016, but currently conveys manufacturing expansion.
- **Housing starts** are near levels seen during recessions.
- **Retail sales growth** is near low levels only seen during recessions. Retail sales excluding-autos is even weaker.
- **Credit risk** is "high" due to leveraged lending and oil and gas.

While some U.S. economic growth data are worrisome, the Fed has been talking aggressively about raising rates, which could slow growth further. Hawkish Fedspeak and global growth concerns have also bolstered the dollar to levels not seen since 2003, which threatens to slow U.S. growth further. Nevertheless, the Fed has lowered its official Fed Funds Rate forecasts in its last seven consecutive quarterly forecast reports.

Global Economic Developments and Outlook

While there are risks to the U.S. economy, global growth has also slowed recently — and downside risks are elevated for the global economy. Christine Lagarde, the head of the IMF, highlighted three major downside risks to the global economy in an early April Bloomberg Television interview: weakness in Chinese manufacturing, low commodity prices, and risk for financials.[14] The IMF lowered its global growth forecasts significantly in April 2016, and then lowered them again in July 2016. These downside risks to global growth compound some of the downside risks to U.S. growth. As such, they are likely to remain critical issues going into the 2016 U.S. election season.

In recent quarters, U.S., Chinese, and global manufacturing have remained weak, and economic growth has been tepid. A Chinese manufacturing recession has been going on for about a year and a half, with Chinese PMI data through July 2016 showing contractions in 18 of the prior 20 months. The People's Bank of China (PBOC) has tried to stimulate the Chinese economy, with modest success. Since China fulfills, in part, a role as the world's factory, some of the weakness in China is the result of weak global demand for manufactured goods.

Eurozone manufacturing and growth had been improving, but Brexit presents uncertainty and downside risks to U.K. and Eurozone investment and growth. Oil prices had been supported by a mix of reduced U.S. oil supply, foreign supply disruptions, and the U.S. summer driving season. But, with the end of the 2016 U.S. summer driving season, oil prices came under pressure again.

Purchasing Manager Indices

The most important forward-looking economic indicators are purchasing manager indices (PMIs), which are surveys of purchasing managers at manufacturing firms. These are good data points for assessing growth, because they are easy to understand, and they show in real time what purchasing managers — the people who buy raw materials at factories — are doing.

PMIs are easy to understand, because the breakeven level for the indices is 50. In other words, if purchasing managers are buying more on a monthly basis, a PMI will be above 50, which is indicative of increased production runs for finished goods — and is a precondition for growth. Readings below 50, however, are indicative of monthly contractions. In the graphs on the following pages, I have indicated the breakeven level of 50 with a solid black line.

PMIs are as close to real time as you can get for significant economic data. This is because PMIs are typically released in the first week of the month, following the month in which the data were collected. In the United States, the ISM Manufacturing Index is a critical PMI. For international PMIs, the Chinese Caixin PMI, the Eurozone manufacturing PMI, and the U.K. CIPS Manufacturing index are some of the most important.

Chinese Caixin Manufacturing PMI

There are two Chinese PMIs: a private PMI and a government PMI. Given questions of validity that often accompany Chinese government data, I prefer the private Caixin Manufacturing PMI.

Based on the Chinese Caixin manufacturing PMI, there has been a manufacturing recession going on in China for about a year and a half. Chinese PMI data through July 2016 showed monthly contractions in 18 of the previous 20 months. An improvement in the Caixin Manufacturing PMI in July 2016 was an upside surprise, but improvements may prove difficult to sustain, as global growth risks remain high. Despite weak Chinese PMIs, official Chinese GDP growth figures remain above 6 percent.

Figure 4-10: Chinese Manufacturing PMI[15]

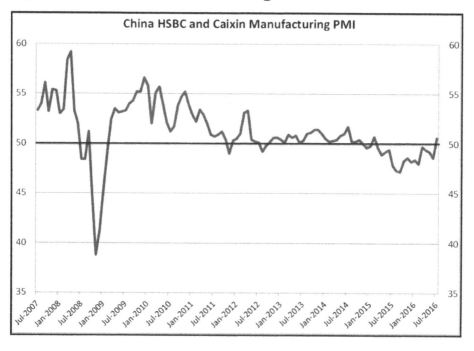

Eurozone Manufacturing PMIs and Growth

Eurozone manufacturing and growth experienced a double-dip recession in the wake of the European sovereign debt crisis. With the implementation of an ECB quantitative easing program at the beginning of 2015, a third recession was averted. Since early 2015, Eurozone manufacturing has trended higher, and the Eurozone economy — in aggregate — had been improving.

The U.K. Brexit vote in June 2016, however, began to present uncertainty and downside risks to Eurozone investment and growth. Plus, additional future referendums that will be held by European Union and Eurozone member countries present further uncertainty and risks of an existential nature for the European Union and the euro.

Figure 4-11: Eurozone Manufacturing PMI[16]

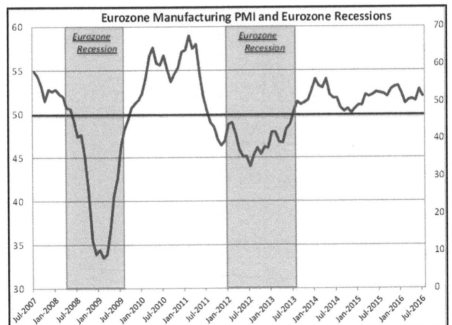

U.K. Manufacturing and Growth

While the U.K. avoided a double-dip recession that plagued Europe in 2012 and 2013, it is likely to slide into recession by the end of 2016, as a result of decreased investment, decreased construction, diminished property values, and slower hiring after the Brexit vote. Manufacturing in the United Kingdom also fell sharply after the Brexit vote in June 2016, as can be seen in the manufacturing PMI (Figure 4-12).

The Brexit vote also substantially weakened the British pound, which is likely to weaken further, as the Bank of England implements monetary accommodation to minimize the extent of a U.K. Brexit recession. Although U.K. growth is likely to slow further, U.K. exports could benefit from a weaker pound.

Figure 4-12: U.K. Manufacturing PMI[17]

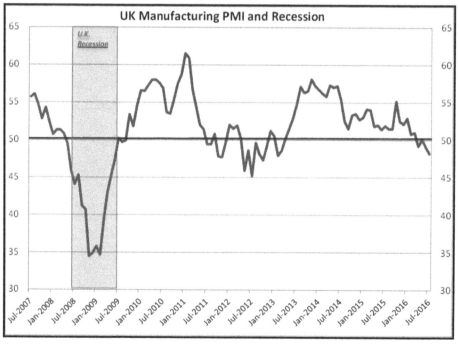

Global Growth Summary

Against a backdrop of downside growth risks to the Eurozone and U.K. economies, low oil and commodity prices have also exerted downward pressure on a number of emerging market economies. The International Monetary Fund (IMF) produces quarterly forecasts of global economic growth, and a 3 percent growth rate is generally accepted as the breakeven for global growth, due to increases in global population. In other words, a global growth rate below 3 percent would generally be indicative of a global recession. The current IMF forecast is for 3.1 percent growth in 2016 (Figure 4-13), which is just above the 3 percent breakeven level. Unfortunately, IMF growth forecasts are notoriously high, and they are frequently subject to downward revisions.

Figure 4-13: IMF Growth Forecasts[18]

IMF Growth Forecasts (July 2016) Annual Forecasts Real GDP, Year-over-Year % Change								
	2010	2011	2012	2013	2014	2015	2016	2017
Global	5.1	3.9	3.4	3.4	3.4	3.1	3.1	3.4
Eurozone	2.0	1.5	-0.7	-0.4	0.9	1.7	1.6	1.4
U.S.	2.4	1.8	2.3	2.2	2.4	2.4	2.2	2.5
Japan	4.7	-0.5	1.5	1.6	0.0	0.5	0.3	0.1
U.K.	1.7	1.1	0.3	1.7	3.0	2.2	1.7	1.3
Canada	3.4	2.5	1.7	2.0	2.5	1.1	1.4	2.1
Brazil	7.5	2.7	1.0	2.7	0.1	-3.8	-3.3	0.5
Russia	4.5	4.3	3.4	1.3	0.7	-3.7	-1.2	1.0
India	10.3	6.6	4.7	6.9	7.2	7.6	7.4	7.4
China	10.4	9.3	7.7	7.7	7.3	6.9	6.6	6.2

Because IMF forecasts are often revised lower, and the July 2016 forecast for total 2016 global GDP growth was 3.1 percent, I believe that the actual rate of 2016 growth will be lower than 3 percent, which would be indicative of a technical recession for the global economy this year. I also expect global GDP will be below 3 percent in 2017. Although this would represent a second year of a technical recession, I do not expect this will be comparable to the Great Recession. I believe the coming recession is likely to be a mild one — like what I am forecasting for the U.S. economy.

Of course, there are downside risks even to my economic outlook. The contagion risks from global oil and gas, Brexit, and other credit concerns for financials present some additional downside risks to my outlook for the U.S. economy and the global economy.

Upside risks for the global economy are heavily predicated on global monetary policies of a stimulative nature. In other words, growth is likely to be reliant on continued quantitative easing, rather than fundamental strength. Meanwhile, the downside risks to global growth lie with fundamental weaknesses in the global economy. As the 2016 U.S. presidential election approaches, the global economy faces fundamental downside risks.

CHAPTER 5

FINANCIAL MARKETS AHEAD OF THE 2016 ELECTION

In addition to looking at the economic impact of U.S. presidential elections, I wanted to examine the impact of presidential elections on financial markets. This is an area that has been well worn for equity markets — especially for the immediate impact in the months following an election. What I have found lacking, however, is a longer-term analysis of the impact of presidential election outcomes on equity markets. I have also found a lack of analysis about the impact of the outcome of U.S. presidential elections on the dollar, oil prices, silver prices, and gold prices.

This chapter tees up the analysis in Chapter 7, which looks at the impact of presidential elections on financial markets, including the Dow, the dollar, oil prices, silver prices, and gold prices. Of course, before we can perform an analysis of the impact of presidential election outcomes on financial markets, we need to look at the current state of these markets.

The Dow Jones Industrial Average

The Dow Jones Industrial Average is comprised of 30 equities, which are some of the largest public companies in the United States. These companies generally have some of the best cash positions and some of the best access to credit. The Dow usually falls during recessions. But the Dow can be resilient — and even strong — ahead of a recession, since Dow companies often serve as a flight to quality for equity investors. The same cannot be said for the NASDAQ index, for example.

The Dow has experienced choppy trading since the spring of 2015, although the Dow was near all-time highs in August 2016, as can be seen in Figure 5-1.

Figure 5-1: Dow Jones Industrial Average[1]

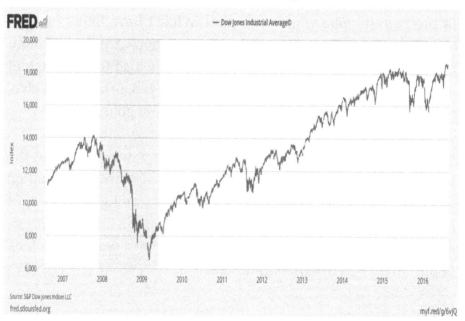

The S&P 500

The S&P 500 is comprised of 500 large equity names traded on U.S. stock exchanges. The index can be more volatile than the Dow, and usually falls during a recession as well. At the time of this book's publication (August 2016), the S&P 500 was near all-time highs, as seen in Figure 5-2.

Figure 5-2: S&P 500[2]

The Dollar

There are a few different ways that the dollar is presented financially as a basket against major currencies, including the NYBOT dollar index (DXY) and the Bloomberg dollar (BBDXY). The Federal Reserve also has its own measure of the dollar known as the trade-weighed dollar, which I have used in this book for analytical purposes. The trade-weighted dollar is defined by the Fed as "a weighted average of the foreign exchange value of the U.S. dollar against a subset of the broad index currencies…. Major currencies index includes the Euro Area, Canada, Japan, United Kingdom, Switzerland, Australia, and Sweden."[3] At the time this book was written, the dollar was at relatively high levels not seen since 2003, as can be seen in Figure 5-3.

Figure 5-3: Trade-Weighted U.S. Dollar (Major Currencies)[4]

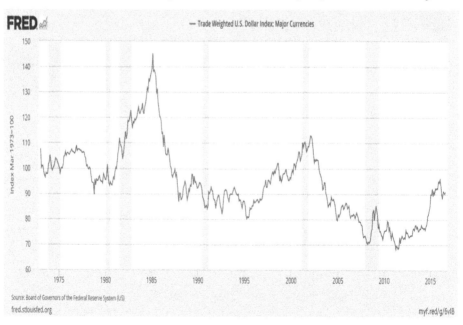

Gold Prices

Gold prices have generally trended higher since the end of Bretton Woods in the early 1970s. Gold prices spiked during the global financial crisis, but subsequently fell, when the dollar strengthened during the period following the European sovereign debt crisis. Gold prices remain relatively elevated, however, considering the level of the greenback, which is at highs not seen since 2003.

At the time this book was written, the price of gold had been trending higher during 2016, as global economic and financial market uncertainty increased, as noted in Chapter 4. I have used nominal monthly gold prices for my analysis, as in Figure 5-4.

Figure 5-4: Nominal Monthly Price of Gold[5]

Silver Prices

Like gold prices, silver prices have generally trended higher since the end of Bretton Woods in the early 1970s. Silver prices spiked during the global financial crisis, but subsequently fell, when the dollar strengthened during the period following the European sovereign debt crisis. Nevertheless, silver prices are relatively elevated, considering the level of the greenback, which is at highs not seen since 2003.

At the time this book was written, the price of silver had been trending higher, as global economic and financial market uncertainty had increased, as noted in Chapter 4. I have used nominal monthly silver prices my analysis, as in Figure 5-5.

Figure 5-5: Nominal Monthly Price of Silver[6]

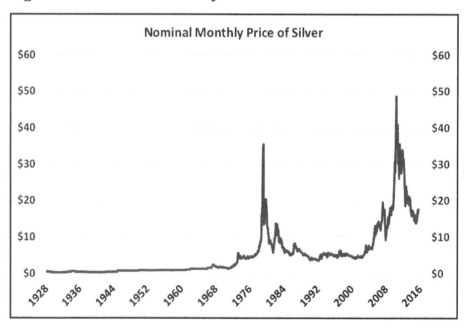

Bretton Woods

On the subject of the dollar, gold, and silver, this is Bretton Woods. Figure 5-6 is a picture of the Mount Washington Hotel, where Bretton Woods is located. This is the hotel where John Maynard Keynes and Harry Dexter White laid out the post-war plans for the global economy in 1944.[7] The Bretton Woods system linking the dollar and gold held until the 1970s, and the end of Bretton Woods has had a profoundly bullish impact on gold and silver prices.

As recently as the 1990s, the Mount Washington Hotel did not have air conditioning, and jackets were required attire in the dining hall. I'll just say that it was not a great place to bring your kids in the summer.

Figure 5-6: Bretton Woods[8]

Crude Oil Prices

Crude oil prices surged ahead of the Great Recession, then collapsed, and then rebounded quickly. Advances in shale drilling technology in the United States allowed new oil supply to come quickly to market, as Eurozone and Chinese manufacturing and growth slowed. Emerging market oil demand growth is critical for oil prices, and with a Chinese manufacturing recession in full swing, oil demand growth has not been as robust, as one would have otherwise expected.

Crude oil prices were under pressure at the time this book was written, and these relatively low crude oil prices posed significant credit risks, as noted by the Fed, FDIC, and OCC in the Shared National Credit reviews of November 2015 and July 2016.

Figure 5-7: Nominal Monthly Price of Crude Oil[9]

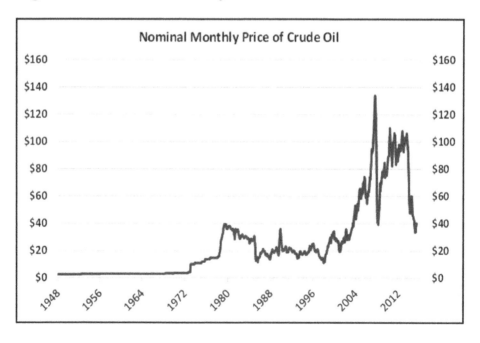

Financial Markets Summary

At the time this book was written, U.S. equity indices were near all-time highs, the dollar was in a high range last seen in 2003, and oil prices were under pressure. At the same time, silver and gold prices has been trending higher.

In Chapter 7, I will examine the impact of presidential elections on these financial markets. Interestingly, the party of each president has generally been less important for financial markets, than it has been for economic indicators.

CHAPTER 6

ELECTION CYCLICALITY AND ELECTION-RECESSION WINDOWS

Welcome to the meaty part of my book. I will share my analysis on how the choice of president has historically impacted the economy and economic indicators. We will begin by looking at the impact on overall U.S. economic growth.

Since the United States has been in an economic expansion since mid-2009, the question on everyone's mind is: when will the next recession start? For this reason, I have focused on the relationship between presidential elections and recession starts. If we look at recessions historically, we are currently in what I like to call an *election-recession window*, which is tied to what I call *election cyclicality* — how elections and business cycles coincide.

Basically, most recessions start in close temporal proximity to U.S. presidential elections. But, before we dig much further into *election cyclicality* and the *election-recession window*, let's quickly look at how the definition of recession has changed, and when recessions have historically occurred.

Recession Defined

Recessions have been traditionally defined by economists as two or more consecutive quarters of negative Gross Domestic Product growth, otherwise known as GDP. During those two or more quarters, the level of GDP falls. This doesn't mean that GDP as a sum of consumption, government spending, investment, and net exports is negative; it means that the level of growth declines, which makes the percent change from one quarter to the next quarter negative.

The National Bureau of Economic Research (NBER) is a recognized authority on business cycle research in the United States, including the timing of U.S. recessions. Since 2010, the NBER has been using a slightly different definition of recession than the traditional definition involving two negative consecutive quarters of growth: "a recession is a significant decline in economic activity spread across the economy, lasting more than a few months, normally visible in real GDP, real income, employment, industrial production, and wholesale-retail sales."[1]

The NBER defines itself as "a private, non-profit, non-partisan organization dedicated to conducting economic research and to disseminating research findings among academics, public policy makers, and business professionals,"[2] according to the NBER website at www.nber.org. The Federal Reserve Economic Database (FRED) of the St. Louis Fed uses the NBER definitions of historical recessions to determine the placement of shaded recession bars on FRED economic and financial market graphs, as seen throughout this book, and especially in Chapter 4 and Chapter 5.

Since the NBER definition of recession is good enough for the Fed, it's good enough for me! I have used the NBER dates and definition of recession throughout this book.

A table of NBER recession dates is on the next page in Figure 6-1, which is followed by an analysis of the relationship between recession starts and presidential elections.

Pre-Election Recessions and Post-Election Recessions
For the purposes of my analysis on the following pages, a **pre-election recession** is defined as a recession that started less than 24 months before a presidential election.

A **post-election recession** is defined as a recession that started less than 24 months following a presidential election, including the recession of November 1948, which started during the month of a presidential election.

Since 1854, there have not been any recessions that started exactly 24 months from a presidential election. So that wasn't a problem in determining if an election should be a pre-election recession or a post-election recession.

As you will see, most recessions have been post-election recessions, the *election-recession window* has narrowed over time. Also, we are in an *election-recession window* right now.

Figure 6-1: Recession Dates According to the NBER[3]

BUSINESS CYCLE REFERENCE DATES

Peak	Trough
Quarterly dates are in parentheses	
	December 1854 (IV)
June 1857(II)	December 1858 (IV)
October 1860(III)	June 1861 (III)
April 1865(I)	December 1867 (I)
June 1869(II)	December 1870 (IV)
October 1873(III)	March 1879 (I)
March 1882(I)	May 1885 (II)
March 1887(II)	April 1888 (I)
July 1890(III)	May 1891 (II)
January 1893(I)	June 1894 (II)
December 1895(IV)	June 1897 (II)
June 1899(III)	December 1900 (IV)
September 1902(IV)	August 1904 (III)
May 1907(II)	June 1908 (II)
January 1910(I)	January 1912 (IV)
January 1913(I)	December 1914 (IV)
August 1918(III)	March 1919 (I)
January 1920(I)	July 1921 (III)
May 1923(II)	July 1924 (III)
October 1926(III)	November 1927 (IV)
August 1929(III)	March 1933 (I)
May 1937(II)	June 1938 (II)
February 1945(I)	October 1945 (IV)
November 1948(IV)	October 1949 (IV)
July 1953(II)	May 1954 (II)
August 1957(III)	April 1958 (II)
April 1960(II)	February 1961 (I)
December 1969(IV)	November 1970 (IV)
November 1973(IV)	March 1975 (I)
January 1980(I)	July 1980 (III)
July 1981(III)	November 1982 (IV)
July 1990(III)	March 1991(I)
March 2001(I)	November 2001 (IV)
December 2007 (IV)	June 2009 (II)

Important Recession Facts from the NBER

As you can see in the table in Figure 6-1, there have been 33 recessions since 1854, which is the oldest date for which the NBER has analyzed business cycles and recessions. For purposes of my analysis, I have only considered these 33 recessions, when evaluating the impact of presidential elections on the business cycle and recession starts.

Recession Starts Since 1854

As I mentioned at the beginning of this chapter, we are most concerned with the timing of recessions starts, since the current U.S. business cycle has gone some time since the last recession started in December 2007.

Of the 33 recessions since 1854, 23 recessions (or 70 percent) started in the 24 months after the election month, and are post-election recessions. Meanwhile 10 recessions (or 30 percent) started before the election month and are pre-election recessions. These data show that a recession is significantly more likely to start in the 24 months after a presidential election, than it is likely to start in the 24 months before.

But, how long after an election is a post-election recession likely to start? In truth: not long at all!

Recession Starts Since 1854

Post-election recessions, which have been 70 percent of recessions since 1854, have had a median recession start only 9 months after a presidential election. The mean recession start for these post-election recessions was 10.5 months after an election.

Similarly, pre-election recessions have tended to start not long before an election. Pre-election recessions, which have been 30 percent of recessions since 1854, have had a median recession start that was 11.5 months before an election. The mean recession start for these pre-election recessions was 12.4 months before an election. These starts can be seen in Figure 6-2.

Recession Starts Since the Great Depression

Some readers may take issue with the recessions that started back in the 1800s. After all, the economy is vastly different now than it was then. The economy was still predominantly agrarian in the mid-1800s, before it transitioned to a manufacturing and industrial economy, and thereafter (and more recently) to a service-sector economy.

You might think that recession starts would be drastically different for a more modern time period — say, since the Great Depression. If you thought so, you might be surprised that the likelihood of a post-recession start has increased, while the timing of recession starts have come closer to elections. Both pre-election and post-election recessions have started closer to presidential elections since 1928 than they did between 1854 and 1928.

There have been 14 recessions since 1928, beginning with the Great Depression that started in 1929, and ending with the Great Recession that started in 2007.

Since 1928, 11 of 14 recessions (79 percent) started after presidential elections. Those post-election recession starts had a median recession start that was only 8 months after a presidential election. The mean recession start for the same recessions was 8.4 months after a presidential election.

Three recessions since 1928 started before presidential elections. These pre-election recession starts had a median recession start that was 10 months before the election. The mean recession start for the same recessions was 9.3 months before the election.

A comparison of pre-election recession starts and post-election recession starts since 1854 and 1928 can be seen in Figure 6-2. As noted previously, the biggest difference is that recession starts have occurred more closely to presidential elections since 1928.

Figure 6-2: Pre-Election and Post-Election Recession Starts

	Pre-Election Recession Starts	Post-Election Recession Starts
	Months Before Election	Months After Election
Since 1854		
Median	11.5	9.0
Mean	12.4	10.5
Since 1928		
Median	10.0	8.0
Mean	9.3	8.4

Election-Recession Window

The time periods before presidential elections and after presidential elections have been filled with recessions. Since most recessions have started historically less than a year before or after a presidential election, I call this period the *election-recession window*.

The bad news is: we are in the election-recession window right now.

Election-Recession Window Narrows

In addition to having a historical *election-recession window,* in which a recession would start during the year before (or more likely) the year after a presidential election, the mean and median start dates of recessions have come closer to presidential elections since 1928. Furthermore, even the outlier recession starts have become less frequent and closer to elections. As such, the *election-recession window* has narrowed.

For all elections since 1854, pre-election recession starts occurred between 1 and 20 months prior to presidential elections. Since 1928, however, the distribution has become tighter, with every pre-election recession starting between 7 and 11 months before a presidential election. Of course, the sample size is smaller since 1928, since there have only been three examples of pre-election recession starts. Nevertheless, the *election-recession window* for pre-election recessions has become much tighter. The same is true for post-election recessions.

For all elections since 1854, post-election recession starts occurred between 0 and 23 months after presidential elections. Since 1928, however, the distribution has become narrower, with every post-election recession starting between 0 and 20 months after a presidential election. Although this range does not look much tighter, the tails on the distribution of post-election recession starts is much wider before 1928.

If we go back to 1854, there have been seven post-election recessions that started more than 13 months after a presidential election, with six of them occurring prior to 1928. Since 1928, however, only one post-election recession has occurred more than 13 months after a presidential election.

Excluding the 1990 Recession
When we look at the post-election recessions since 1928, the recession of 1990 is an exception, because it started much longer after a presidential election (20 months after). If we exclude the 1990 recession, 10 of the 11 post-election recession starts since 1928 occurred between 0 and 13 months after a presidential election. That's 91 percent!

If we look at all post-election recessions back to 1854, that percentage was a much lower 70 percent. And, for post-election recession starts between 1854 and 1928, only 50 percent started in the 13 months following a presidential election. Post-election recessions between 1854 and 1928 were just as likely to start more than 13 months following a presidential election.

***Election-Recession Window* Minimums and Maximums**

The width of the *election-recession window* is determined by the maximum and minimum number of months recession starts have occurred historically in temporal proximity to presidential elections. As I mentioned in the previous section, since 1854, the maximum number of months for a pre-election recession start was 20 months before a presidential election. During that same time period, the maximum number of months for a post-election recession start was 23 months after a presidential election.

Since 1928, however, the election-recession window has narrowed. The maximum number of months for a pre-election recession start was 11 months before a presidential election. During that same time period, the maximum number of months for a post-election recession start (excluding 1990) was 13 months after a presidential election. If we include 1990, the maximum time for a post-election recession start was 20 months after a presidential election. The maximum and minimum number of months recession starts have occurred from presidential elections can be seen in Figure 6-3.

Figure 6-3: Recession Start Month Minimums and Maximums

	Pre-Election Recession Starts Months Before Election	Post-Election Recession Starts Months After Election
Since 1854		
Mininum	1	0
Maximum	20	23
Since 1928		
Minimum	7	0
Maximum	11	20
Max (ex 1990)		13

Election Cyclicality

The coincidence of elections with business cycles is something I call *election cyclicality*. It has two main parts: the *election-recession window* and the *term limit on growth*. As I mentioned in a previous chapter, correlation does not equal causation. Nevertheless, there is a high correlation between the timing of recession starts and elections.

Term Limit on Growth

Since the National Bureau of Economic Research's earliest data on U.S. business cycles in 1854, the maximum number of full presidential terms without the start of a new recession has been two. There have never been three consecutive full presidential terms without a recession start. In this case, I am defining a full presidential term as the four-year period between elections during which one or more individuals may have been president.

Since the last U.S. recession was the Great Recession (starting before President Obama's first term), the conclusion of Obama's second term without a recession start would put us at the historical maximum of two presidential terms without the start of a recession. Two terms without a recession start is the *term limit on growth*. For this reason, I expect that whichever candidate wins the White House in the November 2016 election, he or she is likely to walk into a presidential term with a recession start.

But is the United States really due for a recession?

Based on historical *election cyclicality*, the *election-recession window*, and the *term limit on growth*: Yes.

President Party Affiliation and Economic Data

As you may have noticed, I have not mentioned the party affiliation of presidents so far in this chapter. This is because *election cyclicality* occurs independently of the president's party. This is not true of other economic data, however. In the remainder of this chapter, I will examine the impact of presidential elections and the party affiliation of winning candidates on economic data other than GDP growth, including unemployment, industrial production, housing starts, and auto sales.

Tenure of Presidency

My analysis in this chapter of economic data is based on evaluating changes that occurred during what I call the **tenure of presidency** or **presidential tenure**. This is the timeframe in the post-war period during which an elected president took office (January) until the last full month of his tenure (December), whether that was at the end of a single term—or at the end of two terms.

Shared Presidential Tenure

I controlled for the shared post-war presidential tenures of JFK & LBJ, as well as Nixon & Ford, by grouping them together. I grouped JFK and LBJ into one administration, since LBJ became president in the first half of JFK's term. I grouped Nixon with Ford into one administration, because Ford became president during Nixon's second term, and Ford was never elected president.

Controlling for the Impact of Previous Presidential Tenure

In my analysis, it was also important to control for the impact of a previous presidential tenure on the state of the economy when a new president was elected. In order to achieve this end, I compared the best and worst figures for economic indicators during the first year of a new presidential tenure with the figures at the end of that presidential tenure, whether it was an individual or shared term.

In comparing how unemployment, industrial production, housing starts, and auto sales changed at the end of a presidential tenure (shared or not), it seemed valuable to compare ending levels to the best and worst levels seen in the first year, because those levels could have been reasonably blamed on — or credited to — a predecessor. Improvements from the worst levels in the first year to the end of a president's term or tenure could reasonably be credited to that president. Similarly, a significant worsening of economic conditions from the best levels in the first year to the end of a new president's term or tenure could also be reasonably attributed to that president.

In my analysis of the impact of presidential elections on financial markets in Chapter 6, a more immediate impact was assumed, given the more rapid response of financial markets, compared to the economy.

Now, let's take a look at unemployment, industrial production, housing starts, and autos sales.

Unemployment

The unemployment rate is one of the most critical U.S. economic indicators, and its changes have been highly correlated with the political party of the president since 1948. In fact, since Truman's election in 1948, the unemployment rate has risen during every Republican presidential tenure, except for Reagan. Conversely, the unemployment rate has fallen during every Democratic presidential tenure since Truman's election in 1948, except for Carter, when the impact was mixed.

The changes in the U.S. unemployment rate from the lowest and highest rates of the first year until the end of a presidential tenure can be seen in Figure 6-4. Decreases in the unemployment rate are in green, as well as underlined and bolded. Increases in the unemployment rate are in red, and Carter's mixed changes have been left unshaded and unbolded in the table.

Figure 6-4: Unemployment and Presidential Tenure[4]

President	Party	Lowest Unemployment Rate in Year 1	Highest Unemployment Rate in Year 1	Ending Unemployment Rate
Truman	D	4.3%	7.9%	**2.7%**
Eisenhower	R	2.5%	4.5%	6.6%
JFK/LBJ	D	6.0%	7.1%	**3.4%**
Nixon/Ford	R	3.4%	3.7%	7.8%
Carter	D	6.4%	7.6%	7.2%
Reagan	R	7.2%	8.5%	**5.3%**
Bush 41	R	5.0%	5.4%	7.4%
Clinton	D	6.5%	7.3%	**3.9%**
Bush 43	R	4.2%	5.7%	7.3%
Obama*	D	7.8%	10.0%	**4.9%**

*Through July 2016

A starker presentation of the change in the unemployment rate during a presidential tenure can be seen more clearly when we compare the percentage point changes from the highest and lowest levels seen in the first year of a presidential tenure (Year 1), with the ending level of unemployment of that presidential tenure. This is seen in the left two columns of Figure 6-5. These columns show the differences in the unemployment rate in percentage points. Since a lower unemployment rate is more positive, negative changes are the most positive for the labor market. I have bolded, underlined, and shaded in green the biggest declines in the unemployment rate in percentage points.

The right two columns in Figure 6-5 show how large a percent change the increase or decrease in the unemployment rate was from the lowest and highest rates in the first year of a presidential tenure (Year 1) to the end of the presidential tenure. I have bolded, underlined, and shaded in green the most positive percent changes in the unemployment rate.

Figure 6-5: Changes in Unemployment Rates[5]

President	Party	Percentage Point Change from Lowest in Year 1	Percentage Point Change from Highest in Year 1	Percent Change from Lowest in Year 1	Percent Change from Highest in Year 1
Truman	D	-1.6%	-5.2%	-37%	-66%
Eisenhower	R	4.1%	2.1%	164%	47%
JFK/LBJ	D	-2.6%	-3.7%	-43%	-52%
Nixon/Ford	R	4.4%	4.1%	129%	111%
Carter	D	0.8%	-0.4%	13%	-5%
Regan	R	-1.9%	-3.2%	-26%	-38%
Bush 1	R	2.4%	2.0%	48%	37%
Clinton	D	-2.6%	-3.4%	-40%	-47%
Bush 2	R	3.1%	1.6%	74%	28%
Obama*	D	-2.9%	-5.1%	-37%	-51%

*Through July 2016

Correlation does not mean causation, but there is an extremely high correlation between changes in the unemployment rate and the party affiliation of a presidential tenure.

There could be any number of reasons why the unemployment rate has usually declined during Democratic presidential tenures, but has usually risen during Republican presidential tenures. This could be, for example, the result of fiscal policies designed to stimulate employment, or it could be affected by a Democratic party focus on workers. It could also be, in the case of Obama, tied to the decline in labor force participation or an increase in the level of total government debt, which has increased significantly during his tenure.

Regardless of the causes behind the correlations between political party and changes in the unemployment rate, it seems likely that, based on this historical data, one could reasonably expect a lower unemployment rate at the end of a tenure of a Democrat than at the end of a tenure of a Republican. Of course, past performance is not indicative of future returns. But, historical data seem to support this thesis.

Based on a long-term, secular decline in labor force participation rates, which pushes the unemployment rate lower, I also generally expect lower unemployment rates over time. Of course, this is not necessarily a positive way to see the unemployment rate decline: job creation is better than a shrinking labor force. But, increases in automation could exacerbate declines in labor force participation. This is a subject I discuss in Chapter 8.

Industrial Production

U.S. industrial production has been higher at the end of every presidential tenure since the Second World War, except for that of George W. Bush. Plus, by some measures, industrial production ended higher even at the end of George W. Bush's tenure. At the end of his second term, industrial production ended 2 percent lower than the best rate in the first year of his presidential tenure, but it also ended 3 percent higher than at the lowest level in the first year of his presidential tenure.

The implication here is that no matter who becomes president, industrial production is highly likely to be higher at the end of their presidential tenure. Given the current recessionary levels of industrial production, this should be even less difficult to achieve.

In Figure 6-6, I have bolded and underlined the three greatest percentage increases of industrial production during presidential tenures. These all occurred under Democrats: Truman, JFK/LBJ, and Clinton.

Figure 6-6: Industrial Production Changes[6]

President	Party	Highest Industrial Production Year 1	Lowest Industrial Production in Year 1	Ending Industrial Production	Point Change from Highest in Year 1	Point Change from Lowest in Year 1	Percent Change from Highest in Year 1	Percent Change from Lowest in Year 1
Truman	D	14.7	13.7	19.9	5.2	6.2	**_35%_**	**_45%_**
Eisenhower	R	20.6	18.9	23.0	2.4	4.1	12%	21%
JFK/LBJ	D	25.9	23.0	39.5	13.6	16.5	**_53%_**	**_72%_**
Nixon/Ford	R	40.7	39.7	47.5	6.8	7.8	17%	20%
Carter	D	50.3	47.2	53.3	2.9	6.0	6%	13%
Reagan	R	53.7	51.8	64.4	10.8	12.7	20%	24%
Bush 41	R	64.6	63.5	66.9	2.2	3.3	3%	5%
Clinton	D	69.1	67.1	96.0	26.9	28.9	**_39%_**	**_43%_**
Bush 43	R	95.4	91.2	93.7	-1.6	2.5	-2%	3%
Obama*	D	91.5	87.4	104.9	13.4	17.5	15%	20%

*Through July 2016

Housing Starts

There is a relatively short amount of historical housing starts data available for analysis, since it only goes back to 1959. Nevertheless, changes in housing starts have been less correlated with the party of a president than other economic indicators.

Carter, Bush 41, and Bush 43 saw the biggest drops in housing starts from the lowest levels of the first year of their presidential tenures to the end of their tenures. Obama saw the biggest increases, although that was due to the depressed level of starts during the Great Recession. Housing starts generally seems to be influenced significantly by a base effect of starts in place at the beginning of a presidential tenure.

There is not a clear implication of how the 2016 election will impact housing starts, based on this somewhat shorter time series of housing starts data. Housing starts have improved during Obama's tenure, but they remain near recession levels. As such, the outlook is mixed for the next presidential term and tenure.

Figure 6-7: Housing Starts Changes[7]

President	Party	Highest Housing Starts Year 1	Lowest Housing Starts in Year 1	Ending Housing Starts	Change from Highest in Year 1	Change from Lowest in Year 1	Percent Change from Highest in Year 1	Percent Change from Lowest in Year 1
JFK/LBJ	D	1429	1166	1548	119	382	8%	33%
Nixon/Ford	R	1769	1229	1804	35	575	2%	47%
Carter	D	2142	1527	1482	-660	-45	-31%	-3%
Reagan	R	1547	837	1563	16	726	1%	87%
Bush 41	R	1621	1251	1227	-394	-24	-24%	-2%
Clinton	D	1533	1083	1532	-1	449	0%	41%
Bush 43	R	1670	1540	560	-1110	-980	-66%	-64%
Obama*	D	594	478	1211	617	733	104%	153%

*Through July 2016

Auto Sales

Changes in lightweight vehicle sales (i.e. auto sales) seem to be relatively uncorrelated with the party of the president in office, but the changes in sales seem to be correlated with a change in presidential tenure.

Auto sales seem to alternate from a relatively high annualized level — over 16 million — at the end of a presidential tenure to a low level at the end of the following presidential tenure.

As such, and in keeping with a relatively short time series of auto sales data, I would generally expect the next presidential tenure (regardless of party) to likely end with a significantly lower level of total light vehicle sales, compared to the level at the end of President Obama's presidential tenure. Of course, this forecast is predicated on the expectation that the level of auto sales at the end of Obama's second term will exceed the lowest and highest levels seen in the first year of his presidency. This seems very likely, however.

Figure 6-8: Auto Sales Changes[8]

President	Party	Highest Auto Sales Year 1	Lowest Auto Sales in Year 1	Ending Auto Sales	Change from Highest in Year 1	Change from Lowest in Year 1	Percent Change from Highest in Year 1	Percent Change from Lowest in Year 1
Carter	D	15.2	14.4	10.9	-4.3	-3.5	-28%	-24%
Reagan	R	12.7	9.1	16.4	3.7	7.3	29%	80%
Bush 41	R	16.5	13.4	13.8	-2.7	0.4	-16%	3%
Clinton	D	15.0	13.0	16.2	1.2	3.2	8%	25%
Bush 43	R	22.1	16.3	10.4	-11.7	-5.9	-53%	-36%
Obama*	D	14.8	9.2	16.7	1.9	7.5	13%	82%

*Through June 2016

Fed Funds Rates and Consumer Inflation

There is a bit of an issue when looking at consumer inflation and the Fed Funds Rate, because they influence each other. This can confound an analysis of the two, as there can be a circular feedback loop.

One thing is clear: the biggest drivers of the Fed Funds Rate and inflation levels have not been presidential elections or the parties of presidential tenures. The biggest driver, and the most likely critical factor for the Fed Funds Rate and consumer inflation, is the proximity to the present.

Generally speaking, inflation has been pushed lower as a matter of policy since the 1980s under Fed Chairman Volcker. With relatively low levels of inflation, low levels of Fed Funds Rates have also been warranted. Although the Fed has massively expanded its balance sheet as a result of three quantitative easing programs, inflation remains relatively low.

If the past were to provide insights for the future, I would expect inflation to remain relatively low during the next presidential tenure. A rise in inflation would represent a significant break in a trend that has been in place since the 1980s, and it would present significant upside risks to commodity and real estate prices, while presenting downside risks to bond prices.

Election cyclicality points to a likely imminent recession, which would likely lead to more accommodative Fed policies, but that is more of a second order impact of the presidential election.

International Economic Implications

International economic dynamics are unlikely to be influenced by the outcome of the U.S. presidential election. No matter who wins the 2016 U.S. presidential election, the risk of continued weak Chinese manufacturing is likely remain in play. Additionally, the existential risks to the European Union and the European Monetary Union from the U.K. Brexit vote are likely to remain unaffected by the outcome of the U.S. presidential election. The U.S. and global credit risks from low oil prices, including the downside growth risks to oil-based and commodity-based economies, are also likely to remain unchanged.

Economic Impact of Mixed Legislative Results

It was my hope that I would find some significant takeaways from analyzing mixed and uniform legislative results. Unfortunately, given the short duration of some time series, there was not enough data with which to demonstrate a markedly different impact on economic indicators than when party control of the legislative houses and the presidency was either split or unified.

Economic Impact Summary

The United States has been in an expansion for over seven years since the end of the Great Recession, and the timing of the next recession start is critical. The two attributes of *election cyclicality* point to the likelihood on an imminent recession.

The last recession started two presidential terms ago, and our analysis of NBER historical data for recessions since 1854 indicates that a recession is likely to start before the end of Obama's second term — or in the next presidential term, which starts in 2017. This is the *term limit on growth*.

While the *term limit on growth* points to the high likelihood of a recession before the end of the next presidential term in 2020, the narrow *election-recession window,* that has been in place since 1928 points to a high probability of the next recession start occurring by the middle of 2017.

While political party affiliation is unimportant for *election cyclicality*, the *election-recession window*, and the *term limit on growth*, it is very important for the unemployment rate and industrial production. Based on historical data, it seems reasonable to expect a higher ending unemployment rate under a Republican presidential tenure and a lower ending unemployment rate under a Democratic presidential tenure.

Auto sales are likely to be lower by the end of the next presidential tenure, while the outlook for housing starts is unclear. Fed policy, inflation, and international economic dynamics are unlikely to be directly affected by the election outcome.

CHAPTER 7

FINANCIAL MARKETS AND PRESIDENTIAL ELECTIONS

We saw in Chapter 6 that the outcome of presidential elections, including the party of presidential tenure, can have a significant impact on economic indicators. In my analysis of financial markets, however, I found a different set of relationships — and almost no correlation between financial market activity and changes in the party of the president.

While my economic analysis looked at the best and worst levels of economic indicators during the first year of a presidential tenure, and compared them to the ending level of that tenure, my financial market analysis compares the changes in financial markets between the month after the presidential election in December, and the November of the next presidential election — as well as the November at the end of the presidential tenure period.

I structured my analysis to look for more immediate impacts of a presidential election on financial markets, because financial markets respond more quickly than the economy.

The Dow Jones Industrial Average
A historical analysis of the Dow shows that the Dow ended higher during 15 of the past 21 presidential terms, if we compare the December level of the Dow in the month after a presidential election with the November of the next presidential election. This can be seen clearly in Figure 7-1. There have been only six times since 1928, in which the Dow ended lower.

<u>Implications</u>

Generally, the Dow has risen between presidential elections, with the Dow rising in 71 percent of the presidential terms between presidential elections since 1928. It fell only 29 percent of the time between presidential elections.

Additionally, only three presidents since 1928 have seen the Dow be lower following the election of their successor (at the end of their tenure) than following their own election to the presidency. These presidents were Herbert Hoover, Jimmy Carter, and George W. Bush, who were presidents during the start of the Great Depression, the oil crisis, and the start of the Great Recession, respectively.

Past performance is not indicative of future returns, but the statistical probabilities are indicative of a stronger Dow by the next presidential election (November 2020), compared to the level we see in the month following the 2016 election (December 2016).

Figure 7-1: Percent Change in the Dow During Presidential Terms Since 1928[1]

President	Party	Dow Percent Change from December after Presidential Election Until November of Next Presidential Election
Hoover	R	-81%
FDR	D	204%
FDR	D	-28%
FDR	D	12%
FDR/Truman	D	13%
Truman	D	60%
Eisenhower	R	62%
Eisenhower	R	20%
JFK/LBJ	D	42%
LBJ	D	13%
Nixon	R	8%
Nixon/Ford	R	-7%
Carter	D	-1%
Reagan	R	23%
Reagan	R	75%
Bush 41	R	52%
Clinton	D	98%
Clinton	D	62%
Bush 43	R	-3%
Bush 43	R	-18%
Obama	D	48%

The Dollar

Unlike other financial instruments, there did not seem to be a predictive pattern for the dollar that was influenced by the political party of the presidential candidate. Plus, U.S. presidential elections, in general, did not have a meaningful predictive impact on the direction of the dollar.

As a Chartered Market Technician looking at a chart of the U.S. trade-weighted dollar in Figure 7-2, I would note that the dollar has been trending lower since February 1985. There has been an unbroken pattern of lower highs, which is a generally bearish price formation. As such, I would expect the dollar to fall on trend from a purely technical standpoint. It also happens to be my current forecast, based on my fundamental Fed policy expectations.

Figure 7-2: Trade-Weighted U.S. Dollar (Major Currencies)[2]

Gold Prices

There have only been three times since the end of Bretton Woods, when gold prices fell from the December immediately after a president was elected, until the next presidential election: Reagan's first term, George H.W. Bush (Bush 41)'s term, and Clinton's second term. This means that the price of gold rose in 7 of the last 10 presidential terms, or 70 percent of the time. This track record favors gold prices to rise on trend through the next presidential term. Given the rising level of U.S. debt, and U.S. entitlement exposures, there are also fundamental reasons to expect higher gold prices over time. I discuss these risks in Chapter 8.

Figure 7-3: Percent Change in the Price of Gold During Presidential Terms Since Bretton Woods Ended[3]

President	Party	Gold Price Percent Change from December after Presidential Election Until November at end of Presidential Term
Nixon/Ford	R	104%
Carter	D	365%
Reagan	R	-43%
Reagan	R	32%
Bush 41	R	-20%
Clinton	D	13%
Clinton	D	-28%
Bush 43	R	62%
Bush 43	R	84%
Obama	D	98%

Silver

There have only been three presidential terms since the end of Bretton Woods, when silver prices fell from the December immediately after a president was elected, until the next presidential election: Reagan's first term, George H.W. Bush (Bush 41)'s term, and Clinton's second term. This means that the price of silver rose in 7 of the last 10 presidential terms, or 70 percent of the time. These are very similar dynamics, as those for gold prices.

Even more bullish, is if we look at presidential tenures since 1928. During that time, there have only been three presidents to see lower silver prices at the time of the presidential election at the end of their tenure: Reagan, George H.W. Bush (Bush 41), and Hoover. This historical pattern presents upside risks for silver prices through the next presidential term and tenure.

Figure 7-4: Percent Change in the Price of Silver During Presidential Terms Since Bretton Woods Ended[4]

President	Party	Silver Price Percent Change from December after Presidential Election Until November at end of Presidential Term
Nixon/Ford	R	111%
Carter	D	322%
Reagan	R	-55%
Reagan	R	-3%
Bush 41	R	-38%
Clinton	D	29%
Clinton	D	-4%
Bush 43	R	69%
Bush 43	R	48%
Obama	D	213%

Oil Prices

Since Eisenhower, from the time a president was elected until the next election at the end of his term, oil prices have ended higher 80 percent of the time. This can be seen in Figure 7-5.

Oil prices have only fallen in three terms, the first term of JFK/LBJ, and in both of Reagan's terms. The declines during Reagan's terms can be attributed to the end of oil crisis.

Figure 7-5: Percent Change in the Price of Crude Oil During Presidential Terms Since Eisenhower[5]

President	Party	Crude Oil Price Percent Change from December after Presidential Election Until November at end of Presidential Term
Eisenhower	R	10%
Eisenhower	R	5%
JFK/LBJ	D	-2%
LBJ	D	5%
Nixon	R	16%
Nixon/Ford	R	290%
Carter	D	159%
Reagan	R	-24%
Reagan	R	-45%
Bush 41	R	25%
Clinton	D	22%
Clinton	D	35%
Bush 43	R	70%
Bush 43	R	33%
Obama	D	115%

If we look at presidential tenure in Figure 7-6, we see that since Eisenhower, Reagan is the only President to see oil prices drop during his entire tenure as president from the month after his election until the next president was elected. This has bullish price implications for crude oil prices.

Based on the historical trend of presidential cycles and oil prices, there appear to be upside risks for oil prices during the coming presidential term. Of course, the currently low level of oil prices, as well as the depressed level of oil and gas investment, are also fundamentally likely to bolster oil prices significantly over the next four years. I expect oil prices will rise in coming years, based on these fundamentals.

Figure 7-6: Percent Change in the Price of Crude Oil During Presidential Tenures Since Eisenhower[6]

President	Party	Crude Oil Price Percent Change from December after Presidential Election Until November at end of Presidential Tenure
Eisenhower	R	16%
JFK/LBJ	D	10%
Nixon/Ford	R	353%
Carter	D	159%
Reagan	R	-62%
Bush 41	R	25%
Clinton	D	77%
Bush 43	R	102%

Summary
I have taken a presidential term and presidential tenure view of the dynamics around how presidential elections affect financial markets. This means that my expectations are predicated on the changes that occur during four-year to eight-year periods after a presidential election. Most financial markets appear to behave independently of the political party of presidential tenures, and markets tend to be driven more by secular trends.

The Dow
There have been a mere handful of cases, when equity markets ended a presidential term or presidential tenure lower. Based on the historical tendency for equities to rise during most presidential tenures and terms, it appears likely that the Dow would be higher at the time of the next presidential election in November 2020, compared to its level in December 2016.

Dollar
Neither the party of presidential candidates, nor presidential elections in general, have a statistically significant impact on the dollar, based on my analysis. From a technical standpoint, there is a long-term pattern of lower highs that has been in place for the greenback since it spiked in 1985. I expect the dollar decline to continue on trend, due to fundamental risks from the rising U.S. national debt and entitlement obligations.

Oil Prices

Oil prices have trended higher for all presidents during their presidential tenures, except for Ronald Reagan. Plus, in 80 percent of all presidential terms since Eisenhower, oil prices ended higher. This presents evidence of upside price risks from this election cycle through the next. Fundamentals are also bullish for oil prices, due to significant underinvestment, and rising global oil demand growth.

Gold and Silver Prices

Gold and silver prices have risen in 7 of the last 10 presidential terms. This presents evidence of upside price risks for both metals through the next presidential term. There are also fundamental reasons to expect precious metals prices will rise over time, including U.S. debt and entitlement risks, which are a topic of discussion in the next chapter.

CHAPTER 8

IMPORTANT CONDITIONS UNLIKELY TO CHANGE

What does the outcome of a Hillary Clinton or a Donald Trump victory look like? Some economic impacts seem to be predictable, based on what we have seen in past cycles for Republican and Democratic presidents. However, a number of very important economic and financial risks are unlikely to change, regardless of who is elected president in November 2016.

U.S. recession risks are elevated, because some U.S. growth data have weakened. Plus, in Chapter 6, we looked at how *election cyclicality,* the *term limit on growth,* and the *election-recession window* feed into the risk of a near-term U.S. recession. These recession risks for the U.S. economy exist regardless of which party takes the White House in November.

In addition to these near-term U.S. recession risks, there are even more critical medium-term and long-term factors that pose significant downside risks to the U.S. economy.

In this section, I address some of the things that are unlikely to change, regardless of which party takes the White House in November 2016. In total, I see four major risk factors that are unlikely to change, but which pose significant medium-term and long-term risks to the U.S. economy.

1.) The U.S. National Debt

2.) Entitlements

3.) Demographics

4.) Automation

Be warned! This section is not for the faint of heart.

I will present three options to help you personally face some of these challenges in Chapter 9.

National Debt

The U.S. national debt is a problem, and it is growing. At $19.4 trillion, the national debt is not a small sum. In fact, it comes out to almost $60,000 for every man, woman, and child living in the United States of America in August 2016.[1] Furthermore, no matter who becomes the next president of the United States, the national debt is likely to rise. Case in point: *Marketwatch* reported in February that "Not one presidential candidate cares about the debt and deficits."[2] Then, in July, the *Wall Street Journal* reported that moves to slash the national debt were "gone."[3] That's bad.

The pace at which the U.S. national debt is increasing has accelerated, and a compounding effect has made the underlying value of our debt skyrocket. It took 205 years for the U.S. national debt to exceed $1 trillion, which happened in October 1981.[4] But, it then took less than five years for the national debt to double to $2 trillion, which happened in April 1986.[5]

The most recent doubling of the U.S. national debt occurred over the past eight years. During that period, the level of U.S. government debt more than doubled from a base of $9.5 trillion in June 2008 to $19.4 trillion in June 2016.[6] That is a lot of debt!

One major negative impact of high national debt, is the drag on potential GDP growth. Plus, the compounded debt exposures increase over time, and are exacerbated by the interest on the debt. Unfortunately, while the U.S. national debt situation is large, the financial situation of U.S. entitlements is much larger — and it is likely to compound U.S. debt problems in coming years.

Total public debt as a percent of GDP spiked during the last two presidential tenures, in part as a result of the Great Recession. Obama's presidential tenure through Q1 2016 has shown a whopping 32 percentage point increase in the percent of total U.S. public debt to GDP, which was at 105 percent at the end of Q1 2016. The percentage point increase during Obama's term is equal to the percentage point increases incurred during both Bush presidential tenures combined (Figure 8-1).

I expect the national debt will rise in absolute terms, and as a percent of GDP, during the next presidential tenure. This is part of a continuing trend higher since 2001 (Figure 8-2). Furthermore, during the next presidential tenure, another recession start is likely, due to *election cyclicality*. Even without a recession, however, the level of the national debt (and the national debt as a percent of GDP) is likely to rise significantly during the next presidential tenure. But, the risks of an imminent U.S. recession increases the likelihood that the debt level and the ratio of debt to GDP will rise during the next presidential tenure.

Figure 8-1: Debt as a Percent of GDP, by Presidential Tenure[7]

President	Party	Election	Starting Debt as a Percent of GDP	Ending Debt as a Percent of GDP	Change to End of Tenure
Nixon	R	1968	37%	34%	-3%
Carter	D	1976	34%	31%	-3%
Reagan	R	1980	31%	50%	19%
Bush 41	R	1988	50%	62%	13%
Clinton	D	1992	62%	54%	-8%
Bush 43	R	2000	54%	74%	19%
Obama*	D	2008	74%	105%	32%

*Through Q1 2016

Figure 8-2: Total Federal Debt as a Percent of GDP[8]

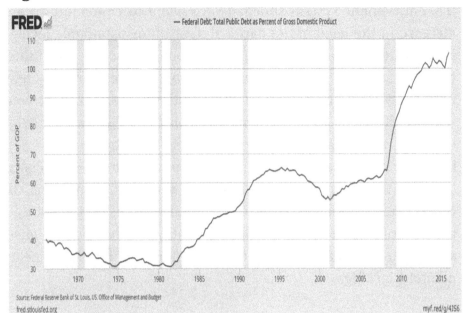

Debt Expectations: Trump and Hillary Tax Plans

The Tax Foundation analyzed the different tax plans and budget proposals of the 2016 U.S. presidential candidates. In its analysis, the Tax Foundation noted that the national debt would rise under Trump.[9] For Hillary, however, the national debt would fall, according to the Tax Foundation's calculations. But, in addition to a decline in the national debt under Hillary's plan, GDP would also contract. It seems unlikely to me, however, that the national debt would be cut at the cost of engendering a recession. As such, I expect that the national debt is not something that will decrease over the next presidential term, regardless of the next president in office. Additionally, U.S. entitlements are likely be an increasingly significant burden for the national budget.

Entitlements

U.S. entitlement system shortfalls are likely to contribute to an increase in the level of the national debt to unsustainable levels. But, entitlements are a third-rail of U.S. politics. I wrote about this critical issue in my book, *Recession-Proof*, but there are very few politicians who are willing to address this issue. Those of you reading this book might be familiar with the TV show, *House of Cards,* in which Frank Underwood (who is played by Kevin Spacey) is the president. As far as I can tell, he is one of the few politicians to really tackle this issue — and he is a fictional character! Of course, real politicians know better than to mess with entitlements. Unfortunately, entitlement obligations are a potential disaster looming ahead, but the political will to face this challenge is painfully lacking.

The total level of all global sovereign debt is currently around 60 trillion dollars.[10] But the size of the off-balance sheet obligations for U.S. entitlements is larger than all of the sovereign debt in the entire world. The total unfunded obligation represented by entitlements was estimated by the Dallas Federal Reserve to be over $100 trillion — back in 2010.[11] More recently, some analyst estimates have put the obligation exposure at over $200 trillion.[12] And that isn't even the bad news!

The Heritage Foundation has taken calculations from the Congressional Budget Office about entitlements to put together Figure 8-3, which is quite catastrophic. This figure shows that by 2030, all U.S. tax revenue, at an unchanged 18.1 percent of GDP, will be consumed entirely by entitlements and the interest on the U.S. national debt.

Figure 8-3: Tax Revenue Spent on Entitlements[13]

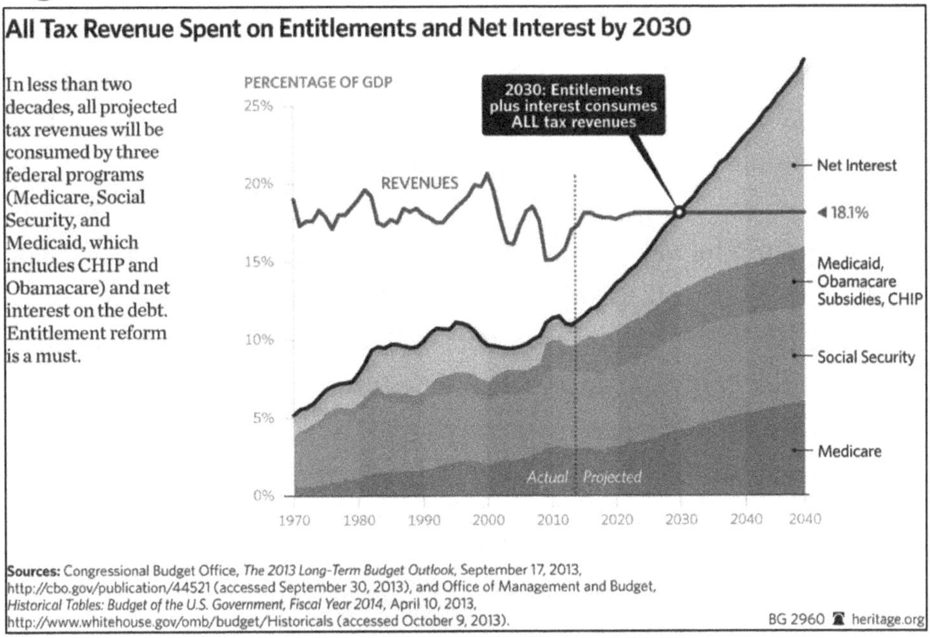
All Tax Revenue Spent on Entitlements and Net Interest by 2030
In less than two decades, all projected tax revenues will be consumed by three federal programs (Medicare, Social Security, and Medicaid, which includes CHIP and Obamacare) and net interest on the debt. Entitlement reform is a must.
PERCENTAGE OF GDP
25%
20%
15%
10%
5%
0%
2030: Entitlements plus interest consumes ALL tax revenues
REVENUES
Net Interest
◀ 18.1%
Medicaid, Obamacare Subsidies, CHIP
Social Security
Medicare
Actual
Projected
1970
1980
1990
2000
2010
2020
2030
2040
2040
Sources: Congressional Budget Office, The 2013 Long-Term Budget Outlook, September 17, 2013, http://cbo.gov/publication/44521 (accessed September 30, 2013), and Office of Management and Budget, Historical Tables: Budget of the U.S. Government, Fiscal Year 2014, April 10, 2013, http://www.whitehouse.gov/omb/budget/Historicals (accessed October 9, 2013).
BG 2960
heritage.org

The U.S. entitlements system is not something that will be easy to fix, and part of the problem with the system lies in its founding.

You see, the grandfather of U.S. entitlements was not LBJ or FDR , it was Otto von Bismarck — a Prussian monarchist. Isn't that a dandy anachronism? Neither Prussians nor monarchists are to be found in abundance, but the system Otto created still exists. Bismarck's portrait is even on the U.S. Social Security Administration's website (Figure 8-3).

Bismarck was a powerful politician known for his use of *Realpolitik,* a political doctrine built on pragmatism to advance national self interests. For him, entitlements were convenient and expedient. Unfortunately, that is no longer the case.

Back in a newly formed Germany, Bismarck was confronted with a rising socialist party, and implementing entitlements could take the wind out of the socialists' sails. In this respect, entitlements were just a means to an end: a way for Bismarck to crush his political enemies inside Prussia and Germany.

But, you might ask: what about the cost of entitlements? See, that's the best part. Bismarck set up the German system to guarantee a pension to workers over 70. But, the average life expectancy in Germany in the late 1880s was only 40.[14] In other words, so few people were expected to receive the benefits, that the program's cost would be negligible. People just didn't live that long.

Figure 8-4: Grandfather of Social Security, Otto von Bismarck[15]

But life expectancy has more than doubled since the 1880s. So, while Bismarck used entitlements to crush his political opponents, the current entitlement system in the United States is a $100 to $200 trillion dollar unfunded liability that threatens to crush the entire U.S. economy. It is neither convenient, nor expedient. Plus, fixing entitlements presents a horrible dilemma, as many Americans rely heavily on entitlements (Figure 8-5).

Figure 8-5: Importance of Social Security for Income[16]

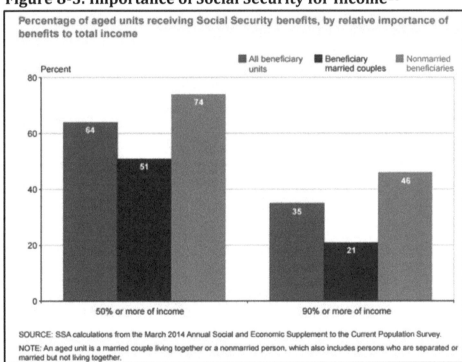

But how did this system break down? Bismarck had such a good thing going. What happened? This can be answered in one word: demographics.

Demographics

Aside from being unable to change the U.S. entitlements situation, the next president will be unable to change U.S. demographics. As life expectancy has increased, birthrates have also fallen. This compounds some of the core problems for entitlements.

U.S. population growth in the United States has fallen from annual rates of over 1.5 percent per year during the 1950s and early 1960s to just 0.7 percent since 2013 (Figure 8-6). Some of this slowing in population growth is due to a decline in the U.S. fertility rate. Fertility rates have fallen in the United States and globally, although the demographer Jonathan Last has noted that the U.S. fertility rate of 1.93 "is exceptionally high. Few industrialized nations are even in the ballpark."[17] This is relative, of course.

Figure 8-6: Annual Population Growth[18]

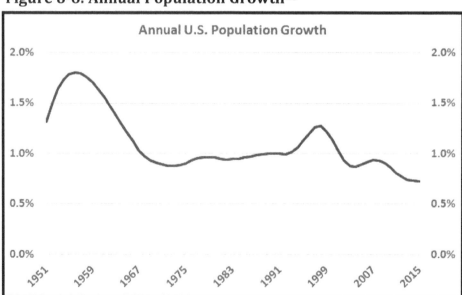

Even though the U.S. total fertility rate is high compared to other industrialized nations, it is below the 2.1 percent "golden number," which is required to maintain a population, according to Last.[19] This is a huge problem for maintaining entitlements. After all, the entitlement system worked really well in 1940, when there were 159.4 workers paying into the system per beneficiary (Figure 8-7), but as of 2013, only 2.8 workers were paying into the system per beneficiary. Plus, the situation is likely to worsen, as the rate falls to 2 workers per beneficiary by 2040.[20]

Figure 8-7: Ratio of Workers to Social Security Beneficiaries[21]

Year	Covered Workers (in thousands)	Beneficiaries (in thousands)	Ratio
1940	35,390	222	159.4
1945	46,390	1,106	41.9
1950	48,280	2,930	16.5
1955	65,200	7,563	8.6
1960	72,530	14,262	5.1
1965	80,680	20,157	4.0
1970	93,090	25,186	3.7
1975	100,200	31,123	3.2
1980	113,656	35,118	3.2
1985	120,565	36,650	3.3
1990	133,672	39,470	3.4
1995	141,446	43,107	3.3
2000	155,295	45,166	3.4
2005	159,081	48,133	3.3
2010	156,725	53,398	2.9
2013	163,221	57,471	2.8

This is a perfect storm for entitlements. On the one hand, U.S. life expectancy has doubled since the first entitlements program was implemented in Germany in 1889 from around 40 years of life to around 80 years. Plus, the age at which people receive entitlements has actually been lowered from 70 to 65. On top of a significantly larger population being eligible to receive entitlements, the medical costs required to support an aging population have risen. In fact, Medicare presents the biggest upside cost risks.

Of course, everything might be ok, if U.S. population growth was extremely robust — but it is not. Population growth has slowed to less than half the rate seen during the Baby Boom years, and total U.S. fertility rate is below the "golden number" that is required to maintain a population. As Last notes, "Social Security is, in essence, a Ponzi scheme. Like all Ponzi schemes, it works just fine – so long as the intake of new participants continues to increase."[22] Unfortunately, that is no longer the case, and entitlements are nearing a breaking point.

One of the big problems with declining demographics is that you have a shrinking tax base, at the same time there are growing entitlement obligations. The unfunded liability of entitlements, which is $100 to $200 trillion (or more) will be borne by an increasingly smaller proportion of the population. On top of this taxation concern, there is another concern about slowing population growth and an aging population: who will do the work, as a growing percentage of the population becomes too old to work.

This answer is simpler: there will be more jobs for robots.

Automation

Just as the next president will be unable to change the trend of U.S. demographics, he or she will be unable to change a trend toward automation. As you will see, automation solves some of the labor shortage risks stemming from demographics, but it is also likely to exacerbate some of the entitlement problems.

As U.S. population growth slows, and older workers age out of the workforce, automation could provide a solution. Automation has the potential to contribute significantly to U.S. economic growth.

When economists discuss the factors that drive growth, they often discuss the three components of the growth model developed by the Nobel Prize winner, Robert Solow.[23] The Solow growth model depicts the drivers of growth in an economy in terms of something called the production function. Basically, this is a just way to conceptualize how growth happens in an economy. It's quite simple really, since there are only three inputs to growth (Y) that matter: capital (K), labor (L), and technology (A). For those of you who like economic formulas, the equation for the Solow growth model is typically written as follows:

$$Y = F(K,L,A)$$

This just means that growth (Y) is a function of capital (K), labor (L), and technology (A). Although A represents technology in this equation, I would argue that, in the future, the A in this equation is likely to increasingly represent automation.

There are two kinds of robots, brain robots and body robots. Both are coming for your job. Unfortunately, neither kind pays payroll taxes, which is the source of entitlements funding. Slowing population growth and the need to automate more jobs is likely to exacerbate debt and entitlement problems, by accelerating the reduction in the U.S. tax base, especially for payroll taxes, which fund entitlements. After all, if entitlements obligations cannot be met with current funding, payroll taxes will rise.

And who pays payroll taxes?

Employees split payroll taxes with their employers, who pay half of payroll tax obligations. So, if entitlements costs send payroll taxes higher, employees will pay more in taxes. It also means that it will cost more for an employer to keep a person employed.

As payroll taxes increase to cover the costs associated with unfunded entitlements, the financial incentives for employers to shift work away from meat-based laborers, and add technology will be incentivized. Some of my clients have already shared with me the concerns about the risk of rising costs associated with Obamacare, for which employers are on the hook — as well as the risk of rising payroll taxes. But, it get worse!

As automation increases, there is likely to be an increasing incentive for employers to automate even more, since robots will unlikely be part of the entitlements tax base. As such, additional automation will pose further upside risks for employer payroll tax obligations, shrinking the entitlements tax base even more.

As you can see, entitlement funding issues incentivize an acceleration in automation, and an acceleration in automation exacerbates entitlement funding issues. It's like the PSA from 1980 about doing cocaine to work longer to make more money, to buy more cocaine, to work longer, to make more money, to buy more cocaine.[24] Except for the United States, the addiction isn't cocaine, its unfunded entitlements that rest on unsound fundamentals, stretching back to a Prussian monarchist.

This is the same problem of "feeding the dragon" that has hurt numerous industries that provided defined benefits retirement plans for their employees (like autos and airlines). Entitlements are the same kind of defined benefits plan, but they don't just threaten one industry with bankruptcy; entitlements threatens the viability of the entire U.S. economy. Private company defined benefits plans were modeled on a demographic structure that was at or near its peak rate of growth. These same challenges threaten U.S. entitlements. Plus, any industry with defined benefits plans is still exposed (like oil and gas).

There is an old joke that the best kind of auto worker to be is a retired auto worker. Soon the joke will be that the best kind of U.S. worker to be will be a retired U.S. worker. This is going to affect all Americans, since the system is an unfunded off-balance sheet obligation, the benefits of which will be reduced drastically for future generations, while the costs to pay in rise further.

Problems beget problems, and automation will be a double edged sword in the fight to stop feeding the dragon.

Stifling Self Employment

Another risk of rising entitlement costs and payroll taxes is that it is likely to stifle entrepreneurship. Self-employed people bear the full brunt of payroll taxes personally, since they do not split the cost with an employer. The self-employment tax rate is currently 15.3 percent.[25] In the future, that rate will rise faster for entrepreneurs, since they will not split the increase in payroll taxes with an employer.

If entitlements are not drastically overhauled, we could see significantly higher self-employment tax rates by 2030. The impact of these additional taxes are likely to engender a continued downward trend in the percent of self-employed workers. According to the Pew Foundation, the percent of employed workers who are self employed has already been in a downtrend, falling from 11.4 percent in 1990 to 10 percent in 2014.[26]

There are also significant implications for the rest of the workforce. According to the Pew Foundation, 30 percent of U.S. jobs are held "by the self-employed and the workers they hire."[27] As such, fewer self-employed would also mean fewer workers hired by the self-employed. Plus, higher self-employment taxes would also hurt workers in the "gig" economy, who — like all 1099s — are also subject to the self-employment tax. This could make the existence of the "gig" economy less tenable as payroll taxes rise.

To understand the potential future impact on employment from financial incentives to automate and outsource, we should look at how manufacturing employment has been impacted.

Manufacturing Jobs

One sector that has already seen a significant amount of automation is manufacturing. Of course, manufacturing has also been subject to a high degree of outsourcing. The number of U.S. manufacturing jobs peaked in 1979, with the number of jobs in manufacturing generally falling on trend since (Figure 8-10).

The 2016 presidential candidates may talk about creating manufacturing jobs or onshoring jobs that have gone abroad, but the only manufacturing jobs that are likely to be created domestically in large numbers are jobs for robots. Automation is likely to continue in manufacturing, and any onshoring of jobs is likely to be to automate jobs that have become labor intensive overseas.

Figure 8-8: Manufacturing Employees[28]

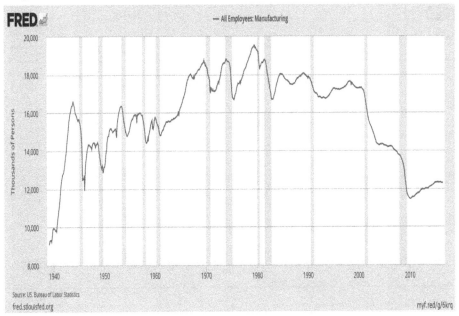

Labor Force Participation

The labor force participation rate is a measure of what percentage of the able-bodied civilian population is working or looking for work. A higher rate shows that more people are engaged in (or trying to) work as a percent of potential workers, while a lower number indicates a smaller percentage of potential workers are engaging in work — and more people are living off the earnings of a smaller percentage of the working population. The labor force participation rate experienced a surge in the 1970s as women entered the workforce (Figure 8-9). Unfortunately, the U.S. labor force participation rate has fallen sharply since it peaked in 2000. I expect further sharp declines as Obamacare and entitlement costs incentivize automation.

Figure 8-9: Civilian Labor Force Participation Rate[29]

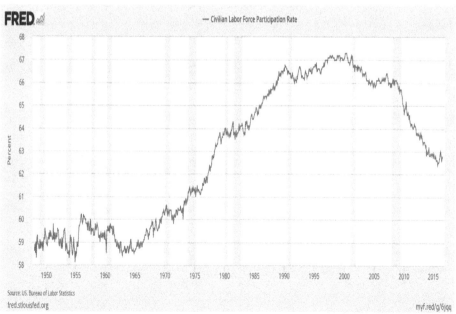

Youth Labor Force Participation

The labor force participation rate for workers aged 16-19 is particularly dismal — and near all-time lows. The rate has been falling since it peaked in 1979, but it has fallen sharply since 2000 (Figure 8-10). Although some analysts and economists note that the increased attainment of higher education is delaying workforce participation, that is not the entire picture. After all, labor force participation rates for workers age 20 to 24 have fallen on trend since 2001,[30] and labor force participation rates for workers age 25 to 54 have fallen on trend since 1999.[31]

In addition to the threats from automation, I also expect youth participation rates will continue to fall, as younger workers are crowded out by older workers.

Figure 8-10: Labor Force Participation Rate (Ages 16 to 19)[32]

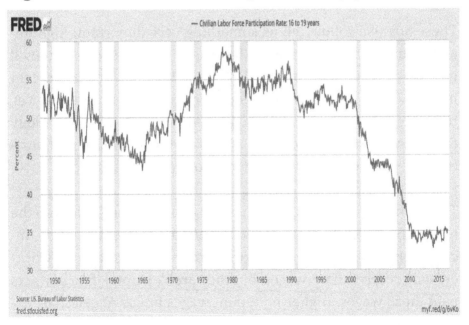

Fast Food Robots Are Coming!

Not all robots look alike. There are brain robots and there are body robots. People use the word artificial intelligence a lot, but this conjures up something way more intelligent than I am talking about. I'm talking about a brain robot as a kiosk — an automated iPad or touchscreen. This is something like you find now at checkouts in most American supermarkets.

In Figure 8-11, you can see what I'm talking about. Here are some fine jobs for robots: automated kiosks. There are no payroll taxes paid on these bad boys, there are no health insurance costs, no government entitlements costs, they don't take vacation, and they aren't in a union. Where are they, you ask? These guys were working hard at the airport in Barcelona, Spain on 2 August 2016.

These Spanish robots tell us something very important: high unemployment rates and spare labor capacity in the workforce will not stave off automation. Spanish unemployment was 20 percent in June 2016,[33] with youth unemployment at 45.8 percent.[34] Yet, there were still jobs for robots. With these kinds of kiosks likely to replace workers, it does not bode well for U.S. youth participation and unemployment rates. Fast food robots are coming!

The push for a higher minimum wage also threatens to hasten the onslaught of fast food robots in the United States. Of course, increases in the minimum wage are extremely beneficial for workers who receive those wages, but they aren't helpful if no one gets paid those wages. Higher minimum wages in Los Angeles, for example, hastened the arrival of robots to do minimum wage jobs.[35] More fast food jobs for robots are coming!

Figure 8-11: Jobs For Robots in Barcelona. How Gaudi![36]

High-End Automation

You might think that kiosks are only coming for minimum wage jobs, and your job is safe. Unfortunately, you are very likely wrong. The underfunded entitlements, which lead to higher payroll taxes, combined with rising Obamacare costs, and potentially accompanied by higher minimum wages are providing incentives for employers to automate all kinds of service sector jobs.

Earlier this year, I was in Jacksonville, Florida for a conference. On my way back to Austin, I saw the ad below (Figure 8-12) hanging in the Jacksonville airport. I was shocked. I thought the concept of automation in finance was unknown to most people.

I realized when I saw this poster in the Jacksonville airport that automation is already completely ingrained in the American *Zeitgeist*. We know the robots are coming for our jobs. We just haven't fully accepted it yet — and we are woefully unprepared.

Figure 8-12: Jobs For Robots in Jacksonville, Florida[37]

Summary

Some of the biggest challenges facing the American economy in the next decade have not even been discussed by the presidential candidates. The national debt is a non-issue, entitlement obligations of $100 to $200 trillion are a hush-hush third rail, while demographics threaten to reduce the U.S. tax base, force payroll taxes higher, and choke off entrepreneurship.

Automation is a deal with the devil, since it is financially incentivized by risks of increased payroll taxes, increased Obamacare costs, and higher minimum wage rates. Yet, automation accelerates the funding problems of the national defined benefits program (e.g. entitlements) that only worked when the age at which one received benefits exceeded life expectancy by 30 years. Robots and automation can solve the shrinking population problem, but they are likely to exacerbate the problem of a shrinking tax base, especially for entitlements.

The acceleration of automation is also likely to drive labor force participation rates significantly lower during the next economic downturn. Labor force participation rates are already at the lowest rates since the 1970s, and youth labor force participation rates are near all-time lows. But, they are likely to fall further to new all-time lows, as younger and less-experienced workers lose out when more jobs for robots are created. Higher end jobs are also exposed.

A broader discussion of automation will be the focus of my next book Jobs For Robots, which will be out in February 2017.

CHAPTER 9

RESPONDING TO RISKS AND CHALLENGES

We have looked at the impact of presidential elections on financial markets and the economy in this book, although some of the most important economic and financial market risks for the average reader are not dependent on which party controls the White House. The most important issues have already been set in stone. In the near-term, *election cyclicality* and the weakness of recent economic data underscore the risks of a recession start in the near term. But, bigger problems of debt, entitlements, demographics, and automation are lurking around the corner.

Tectonic and Teacup Economics
The steady stream of U.S. economic data are critical for presidential candidates ahead of an election, and they fill Twitter feeds and blog posts. But these changes in the U.S. economy can be minor, compared to some of the larger risks I have discussed in the previous chapter. An economist I used to work with liked to say that the economy often looked good on the surface, but tectonic plates underneath threatened to upend the apparent calm.

While the tectonic plate analogy is a good one, I like to describe the risks as *teacup economics*. Maybe you've been to Disney World, or a similar theme park, where they have a teacup ride (Figure 9-1). You sit in a chair shaped like a teacup, with a small table that you hold on to. The teacup spins and spins and spins.

Balancing the current economic conditions against the medium-term and long-term risks to the U.S. economy is like playing chess on the teacup ride. The current economic conditions are like a chessboard set on the little table in the middle of the teacup, while the spinning force represents the underlying medium-term and long-term risks to the economy. The board is set, and it might hold for some time, but there are bigger factors that are likely to send the system spinning — and make the game end quickly.

Figure 9-1: Teacup Economics[1]

When I was kid, I loved the Teacup ride. I still enjoyed it when I was a certified interpreter at Disney World during college, but it was more fun as a kid. When I think about that ride as an analogy for the economy now, it does make me a bit nauseous!

But, you and I have options, and I've laid out three in this chapter.

Option #1: Get Vocal
Because some of the biggest risks to the U.S. economy are not on the radar of most politicians, one way to address the issues that concern you is to get civically involved. Regardless of your party affiliation, if these issues concern you, contact your government representatives. Personally, I like to call the White House comment line.

Here's the number:

202-456-1111

I can't guarantee it, but I expect there is some kind of algorithm politicians use to evaluate constituent sentiment that is influenced by touchpoints. In other words, when you reach out there is a kind of leverage for your outreach. Since there is likely an equation to determine how many people didn't reach out, but who also cared about a certain issue.

According to Peter and Hull in *The Peter Principle*: "A political party is usually naively pictured as a group of like-minded people operating to further their common interests. This is no longer valid. That function is now carried on entirely by *the lobby*, and there are as many lobbies as there are special interests."[3] Become one of those special interests. Your political representatives' contact info is here: https://www.usa.gov/elected-officials

Option #2: Manage Your Finances

I was at an invitation-only offsite of the Atlanta Fed a number of years ago, when I heard an expert from a think-tank note that the only way to solve the U.S. debt and entitlements issues was by a two-pronged approach of repression and inflation. The inflation component of this equation is clear, but the repression component may not be. The punchline, is that the government might eventually mandate that tax-advantaged retirement accounts (like IRAs and 401Ks) be required to hold government Treasuries. This would open up U.S. debt to an entirely new (and captive) pool of capital — but it could be a disaster for investors.

A client of mine is a very serious investment banker. He is one of the top guys in his field, and this very serious and senior investment banking managing director converted his investments to an annuity, because he has more faith in an insurance company to pay out the annuity, than he has trust in the U.S. government not to seize his retirement account at some point. He may be right!

I'm not recommending this,[3] but I think it's critical for you to know that serious people in finance and banking have very real concerns that a government mandate on Treasury purchases is going to happen at some point. If we do not fix the debt and entitlements situation, this is a very real possibility.

From a risk management standpoint, annuities and physical assets would be tougher for the U.S. government to seize or direct if it needed to sell more Treasuries. And it *will* need to sell more.

As we saw in Chapter 8, by 2030, the entire U.S. tax budget (as a percent of GDP) is expected to cover just the cost of entitlements and the interest on the U.S. national debt.

Option #3: Manage Your Career (and read *Recession-Proof*)
I spent a great deal of time in my last book, *Recession-Proof*, discussing how to best manage your career — especially in uncertain economic times. No matter how big the economic risks, there are always some industries that will be evergreen.

In light of the aging U.S. population, healthcare is likely to remain a huge opportunity professionally. In fact, one of the biggest concerns of auto parts manufacturers at a conference I spoke at in Chicago in April 2016 was Obamacare – not recession, not China, not entitlements. It was the cost of Obamacare. This threatens to hasten automation, as I mentioned in the last chapter, but it also highlights the upside costs and opportunities in healthcare. This is also further reinforced by the spread between categories of entitlements, and the expected and forecasted rates of growth for costs of healthcare entitlements — especially Medicare.

While entitlements and demographics may threaten a number of industries with automation, healthcare is likely to remain evergreen, as a more difficult sector to automate for sometime to come. In fact, any industry where you need person-to-person contact is likely to remain relatively safe. As such, a career in healthcare or care-giving is likely to be a solid option for some time.

In addition to the opportunities presented by the healthcare sector, there are also likely to be some significant opportunities in information technology — especially automation.

I recently had a call with a former colleague (and good friend) who works for a company at the forefront of vehicle automation. I was talking to him about the risks to the economy and financial markets due to my expectations of a recession. He was very concerned, because part of his compensation is tied to the performance of the NASDAQ.

I told him, "you have nothing to worry about." Then, he asked me why. I was laughing as I told him, "The stock market may fall, but you're going to be the last guy on earth with a job. Literally. The. Last. Guy. It's your job to automate every other job out of existence. You're going to be just fine!" He was happy with that answer. If you can find a gig in automation, you'd probably be pretty happy with your prospects as well.

By the way, I have followed my own advice about gaining professional exposure to automation. In fact, my company, Prestige Economics, has a five-year forecasting and modeling agreement with MHI, the material handling industry and trade organization in the United States. This is a multi-billion dollar industry that provides the physical equipment and technology that moves goods through the U.S. supply chain. It also happens to be an industry that, in part, is focused on automation. Basically, I'm just trying to be the second-to-last guy on earth with a job.

Who Should You Vote For?
There are a lot of different reasons people vote for a political candidate. Based on the historical data and *election cyclicality*, as well as recent economic indicators, the near-term economic outlook for a recession looks pretty much baked in.

I'm not a political pundit, and there are a lot of different reasons to vote for a presidential candidate. But, after looking at the data, it appears that the choice of president is going to be less important for near-term economic implications. As such, you may wish to consider voting for the candidate that you believe has the highest probability of addressing long-term risks, like entitlements, which pose an existential threat to the U.S. economy.

If you still aren't sure who to vote for, don't worry about it. After all, based on *election cyclicality*, you'll be electing recession either way!

END NOTES

Chapter 2

1. The full list of parties can be found here: https://ballotpedia.org/List_of_political_parties_in_the_United_States

2. There have been exceptions. See the maps at http://www.270towin.com/historical-presidential-elections/

3. http://www.history.com/topics/us-presidents/andrew-jackson and http://www.history.com/topics/jacksonian-democracy

4. I have licensed this image with permission from the National Portrait Gallery in London, England.

5. http://www.nytimes.com/interactive/2016/08/01/us/elections/nine-percent-of-america-selected-trump-and-clinton.html?_r=0

6. Peter, L. and Hull, R. (2009). *The Peter Principle*. New York: Harper Collins, p. 57.

7. Ibid.

8. Ibid, 56.

9. http://www.270towin.com/

Chapter 3

1. Craig, G. (1980). *Germany 1846-1945*. New York: Oxford University Press. pp. 315-317.

2. http://www.270towin.com/

3. http://www.cnn.com/POLITICS/pollingcenter/ Retrieved on 28 October 2012

4. This chapter is my own analysis of the historical maps for U.S. presidential elections at http://www.270towin.com/

5. Check out the Washington Post article, "RIP 'American Idol': The show that proved how bad Americans are at voting." It even has a graph showing voter turnout in U.S. presidential elections versus American Idol. I couldn't make this stuff up if I tried:

6. https://www.washingtonpost.com/news/the-fix/wp/2015/05/11/rip-american-idol-the-show-that-gave-us-an-easy-shorthand-for-americans-not-voting/

Chapter 4

1. https://fred.stlouisfed.org/

2. US. Bureau of Economic Analysis, Gross Domestic Product [GDP], retrieved from FRED, Federal Reserve Bank of St. Louis; https://fred.stlouisfed.org/series/GDP, August 11, 2016.

3. US. Bureau of Economic Analysis, Real Gross Domestic Product [GDPC1], retrieved from FRED, Federal Reserve Bank of St. Louis; https://fred.stlouisfed.org/series/GDPC1, August 11, 2016.

4. US. Bureau of Labor Statistics, Civilian Unemployment Rate [UNRATE], retrieved from FRED, Federal Reserve Bank of St. Louis; https://fred.stlouisfed.org/series/UNRATE, August 11, 2016.

5. US. Bureau of Labor Statistics, Consumer Price Index for All Urban Consumers: All Items [CPIAUCSL], retrieved from FRED, Federal Reserve Bank of St. Louis; https://fred.stlouisfed.org/series/CPIAUCSL, August 17, 2016.

6. Board of Governors of the Federal Reserve System (US), Industrial Production Index [INDPRO], retrieved from FRED, Federal Reserve Bank of St. Louis; https://fred.stlouisfed.org/series/INDPRO, August 17, 2016.

7. Institute of Supply Management. Retrieved from FRED, Federal Reserve Bank of St. Louis; July 2016.

8. US. Bureau of Economic Analysis, Light Weight Vehicle Sales: Autos and Light Trucks [ALTSALES], retrieved from FRED, Federal Reserve Bank of St. Louis; https://fred.stlouisfed.org/series/ALTSALES, August 11, 2016.

9. US. Bureau of the Census, Housing Starts: Total: New Privately Owned Housing Units Started [HOUST], retrieved from FRED, Federal Reserve Bank of St. Louis; https://fred.stlouisfed.org/series/HOUST, August 17, 2016.

10. Board of Governors of the Federal Reserve System (US), Effective Federal Funds Rate [DFF], retrieved from FRED, Federal Reserve Bank of St. Louis; https://fred.stlouisfed.org/series/DFF, August 11, 2016.

11. https://www.federalreserve.gov/newsevents/press/bcreg/20151105a.htm

12. http://www.federalreserve.gov/newsevents/press/bcreg/20160729a.htm

13. Ibid.

14. http://www.bloomberg.com/news/videos/2016-04-05/lagarde-brexit-part-of-2016-geopolitical-uncertainty

15. Chinese Manufacturing PMI data sourced from www.econoday.com

16. Eurozone Manufacturing PMI data sourced from www.econoday.com

17. U.K. CPIS Manufacturing PMI data sourced from www.econoday.com

18. http://www.imf.org/external/pubs/ft/weo/2016/update/02/pdf/0716.pdf

Chapter 5

1. S&P Dow Jones Indices LLC, Dow Jones Industrial Average© [DJIA], retrieved from FRED, Federal Reserve Bank of St. Louis; https://fred.stlouisfed.org/series/DJIA, August 10, 2016.

2. S&P Dow Jones Indices LLC, S&P 500© [SP500], retrieved from FRED, Federal Reserve Bank of St. Louis; https://fred.stlouisfed.org/series/SP500, August 10, 2016.

3. Board of Governors of the Federal Reserve System (US), Real Trade Weighted U.S. Dollar Index: Major Currencies [TWEXMPA], retrieved from FRED, Federal Reserve Bank of St. Louis; https://fred.stlouisfed.org/series/TWEXMPA, August 11, 2016.

4. Ibid.

5. London Bullion Market Association, Bureau of Labor Statistics as sourced from MacroTrends Data.

6. London Bullion Market Association, Bureau of Labor Statistics as sourced from MacroTrends Data.

7. Steil, B. (2013). *The Battle of Bretton Woods.* Princeton, NJ: Princeton University Press, pp. 1-15.

8. Personal Photo Collection of Janet Schenker.

9. Energy Information Administration, Bureau of Labor Statistics as sourced from MacroTrends Data.

Chapter 6

1. Definition of recession. http://www.nber.org/cycles.html

2. About the NBER. http://www.nber.org/info.html

3. All of the calculations in this chapter come from an analysis of this table. http://www.nber.org/cycles.html

4. US. Bureau of Labor Statistics, Civilian Unemployment Rate [UNRATE], retrieved from FRED, Federal Reserve Bank of St. Louis; https://fred.stlouisfed.org/series/UNRATE, August 11, 2016.

5. Ibid.

6. Board of Governors of the Federal Reserve System (US), Industrial Production Index [INDPRO], retrieved from FRED, Federal Reserve Bank of St. Louis; https://fred.stlouisfed.org/series/INDPRO, August 17, 2016.

7. US. Bureau of the Census, Housing Starts: Total: New Privately Owned Housing Units Started [HOUST], retrieved from FRED, Federal Reserve Bank of St. Louis; https://fred.stlouisfed.org/series/HOUST, August 17, 2016.

8. US. Bureau of Economic Analysis, Light Weight Vehicle Sales: Autos and Light Trucks [ALTSALES], retrieved from FRED, Federal Reserve Bank of St. Louis; https://fred.stlouisfed.org/series/ALTSALES, August 11, 2016.

Chapter 7

1. London Bullion Market Association, Bureau of Labor Statistics as sourced from MacroTrends Data.

2. Board of Governors of the Federal Reserve System (US), Real Trade Weighted U.S. Dollar Index: Major Currencies [TWEXMPA], retrieved from FRED, Federal Reserve Bank of St. Louis; https://fred.stlouisfed.org/series/TWEXMPA, August 11, 2016.

3. London Bullion Market Association, Bureau of Labor Statistics as sourced from MacroTrends Data.

4. London Bullion Market Association, Bureau of Labor Statistics as sourced from MacroTrends Data.

5. Energy Information Administration, Bureau of Labor Statistics as sourced from MacroTrends Data.

6. Personal Photo Collection of Janet Schenker.

7. Energy Information Administration, Bureau of Labor Statistics as sourced from MacroTrends Data.

Chapter 8

1. http://www.brillig.com/debt_clock/

2. http://www.marketwatch.com/story/not-one-presidential-candidate-cares-about-the-debt-and-deficits-2016-02-

3. http://www.wsj.com/articles/debate-over-u-s-debt-changes-tone-1469385857

4. Bloomberg Professional Service.

5. Ibid.

6. Ibid.

7. Federal Reserve Bank of St. Louis and US. Office of Management and Budget, Federal Debt: Total Public Debt as Percent of Gross Domestic Product [GFDEGDQ188S], retrieved from FRED, Federal Reserve Bank of St. Louis; https://fred.stlouisfed.org/series/GFDEGDQ188S, August 11, 2016.

8. Ibid.

9. Sourced from the Tax Foundation. http://taxfoundation.org/blog/comparison-presidential-tax-plans-and-their-economic-effects

10. http://www.visualcapitalist.com/60-trillion-of-world-debt-in-one-visualization/

11. http://www.dallasfed.org/news/speeches/fisher/2010/fs100210.cfm: "According to our calculations at the Dallas Fed, that unfunded debt of Social Security and Medicare combined has now reached $104 trillion—trillion with a 'T'—in discounted present value."

12. http://www.usnews.com/opinion/economic-intelligence/2015/11/18/social-security-and-medicare-have-morphed-into-unsustainable-entitlements

13. The Heritage Foundation. Sourced from http://thf_media.s3.amazonaws.com/infographics/2014/10/BG-eliminate-waste-control-spending-chart-3_HIGHRES.jpg

14. See page 315 at http://www.nber.org/chapters/c7434.pdf

15. Social Security Administration. Sourced from https://www.ssa.gov/history/ottob.html

16. Social Security Administration. Sourced from https://www.ssa.gov/policy/docs/chartbooks/fast_facts/

17. Last, J. (2013) *What to Expect, When No One's Expecting: America's Coming Demographic Disaster.* New York: Encounter Books.,p6.

18. Bloomberg Professional Service.

19. Last (2013), p.4.

20. Ibid., p. 109.

21. Social Security Administration. Sourced from https://www.ssa.gov/history/ratios.html. Last (2013) also uses a similar table in his book on page 108.

22. Last (2013), p. 107.

23. For more information on Solow, you can read a full lecture on Solow and the Solow growth model here: http://facstaff.uww.edu/ahmady/courses/econ302/lectures/Lecture14.pdf

24. PSA Partnership for a Drug-Free America - So I can do more coke (1980). Retrieved from: http://lybio.net/tag/im-always-chasing-rainbows-psa-remarks/ https://www.youtube.com/watch?v=XGAVTwhsyOs

25. https://www.irs.gov/businesses/small-businesses-self-employed/self-employment-tax-social-security-and-medicare-taxes

26. Washington Post. https://www.washingtonpost.com/business/capitalbusiness/minimum-wage-offensive-could-speed-arrival-of-robot-powered-restaurants/2015/08/16/35f284ea-3f6f-11e5-8d45-d815146f81fa_story.html

27. Ibid.

28. US. Bureau of Labor Statistics, All Employees: Manufacturing [MANEMP], retrieved from FRED, Federal Reserve Bank of St. Louis; https://fred.stlouisfed.org/series/MANEMP, August 11, 2016.

29. US. Bureau of Labor Statistics, Civilian Labor Force Participation Rate [CIVPART], retrieved from FRED, Federal Reserve Bank of St. Louis; https://fred.stlouisfed.org/series/CIVPART, August 11, 2016.

30. US. Bureau of Labor Statistics, Civilian Labor Force Participation Rate: 20 to 24 years [LNS11300036], retrieved from FRED, Federal Reserve Bank of St. Louis; https://fred.stlouisfed.org/series/LNS11300036, August 10, 2016.

31. US. Bureau of Labor Statistics, Civilian Labor Force Participation Rate: 25 to 54 years [LNS11300060], retrieved from FRED, Federal Reserve Bank of St. Louis; https://fred.stlouisfed.org/series/LNS11300060, August 11, 2016.

32. US. Bureau of Labor Statistics, Civilian Labor Force Participation Rate: 16 to 19 years [LNS11300012], retrieved from FRED, Federal Reserve Bank of St. Louis; https://fred.stlouisfed.org/series/LNS11300012, August 10, 2016.

33. http://www.tradingeconomics.com/spain/unemployment-rate

34. http://www.tradingeconomics.com/spain/youth-unemployment-rate

35. https://www.washingtonpost.com/business/capitalbusiness/minimum-wage-offensive-could-speed-arrival-of-robot-powered-restaurants/2015/08/16/35f284ea-3f6f-11e5-8d45-d815146f81fa_story.html

36. Personal Photo Collection of Jason Schenker.

37. Ibid.

Chapter 9

1. Personal Photo Collection of Janet Schenker.

2. Peter and Hull (2009), p. 58.

3. I am actually not making any explicit recommendations or giving investment advice. Please see the disclaimers in the back of the book.

AUTHOR

ABOUT THE AUTHOR

Jason Schenker is the President and Chief Economist of the financial market research and consulting firm, Prestige Economics, LLC. Mr. Schenker writes market commentary, produces forecasts, manages Prestige Economics consulting projects, and is the author of multiple books. He has been a Guest Columnist for Bloomberg News and a Guest Host of the Bloomberg Television show "Street Smart."

Mr. Schenker holds a master's degree in Applied Economics from The University of North Carolina-Greensboro, a Master's Degree in Negotiation and Conflict Resolution from California State University-Dominguez Hills, a master's degree in Germanic Languages and Literature from The University of North Carolina-Chapel Hill, and a bachelor's degree with distinction in History and German from The University of Virginia. Mr. Schenker also holds the professional designations of CMT® (Chartered Market Technician), CFP® (Certified Financial Planner), CVA® (Certified Valuation Analyst), and ERP® (Energy Risk Professional).

Mr. Schenker previously held roles with McKinsey and Company as a Risk Specialist and at Wachovia Corporation as the Chief Energy and Commodity Economist. Bloomberg News has ranked Mr. Schenker one of the most accurate forecasters in the world over multi-year periods in 31 different categories for his forecasts of industrial metals prices, precious metals prices, oil prices, natural gas prices, agricultural commodity prices, foreign exchange rates, and U.S. economic indicators.

RANKINGS

TOP FORECASTER ACCURACY RANKINGS

Very few people ever have the privilege to say they are a market leader. I am so proud that my firm, Prestige Economics, has been recognized as the most-accurate independent commodity and financial market research firm in the world since 2010. As the only forecaster for Prestige Economics, these rankings implicitly rank me one of the most-accurate forecasters in the world. In total, Bloomberg News has ranked me a top forecaster in 31 categories through the end of Q2 2016.

In total, I have been ranked a top economic forecaster, energy price forecaster, metals price forecaster, agricultural price forecaster, and foreign exchange rate forecaster.

ECONOMIC TOP RANKINGS
#1 Non-Farm Payroll Forecaster in the World
#2 U.S. Unemployment Rate Forecaster in the World
#3 Durable Goods Orders Forecaster in the World
#7 ISM Manufacturing Index Forecaster in the World

ENERGY PRICE TOP RANKINGS

#1 WTI Crude Oil Price Forecaster in the World
#1 Brent Crude Oil Price Forecaster in the World
#1 Henry Hub Natural Gas Price Forecaster in the World

METALS PRICE TOP RANKINGS

#1 Gold Price Forecaster in the World
#1 Platinum Price Forecaster in the World
#1 Industrial Metals Price Forecaster in the World
#1 Copper Price Forecaster in the World
#1 Nickel Price Forecaster in the World
#1 Tin Price Forecaster in the World
#1 Zinc Price Forecaster in the World
#2 Precious Metals Price Forecaster in the World
#2 Silver Price Forecaster in the World
#2 Palladium Price Forecaster in the World
#2 Aluminum Price Forecaster in the World
#2 Lead Price Forecaster in the World

AGRICULTURAL PRICE TOP RANKINGS

#1 Coffee Price Forecaster in the World

FOREIGN EXCHANGE TOP RANKINGS

#1 Euro Forecaster in the World
#1 British Pound Forecaster in the World
#1 Swiss Franc Forecaster in the World
#1 Brazilian Real Forecaster in the World
#1 Euro/Swiss Franc Forecaster in the World
#2 Euro/Japanese Yen Forecaster in the World
#2 Pound/Euro Forecaster in the World
#2 Russian Ruble/Euro Forecaster in the World
#4 Japanese Yen Forecaster in the World
#5 Major Currency Forecaster in the World
#6 Australian Dollar Forecaster in the World

---- PUBLISHER ----

ABOUT THE PUBLISHER

Prestige Professional Publishing, LLC was founded in 2011 to produce readable, insightful, and timely professional reference books. We are registered with the Library of Congress, and based in Austin, Texas.

Past Titles

Be The Shredder, Not The Shred (May 2012)

Commodity Prices 101 (October 2012)

Future Titles

Commodity Prices 101, Second Edition (November 2016)

Jobs For Robots (February 2017)

The Valuation Onion (August 2017)

RECESSION-PROOF

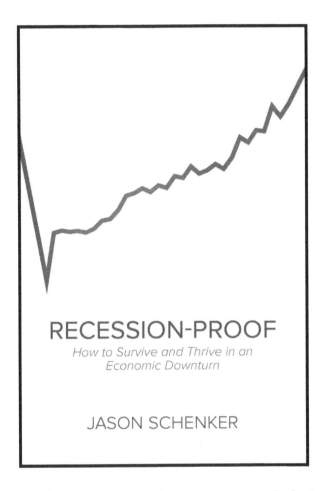

Recession-Proof presents proactive strategies to help individuals survive and thrive in the next economic downturn. Recession-Proof was published by Lioncrest Publishing in February 2016. It has been a #1 Best Seller.

COMMODITY PRICES 101

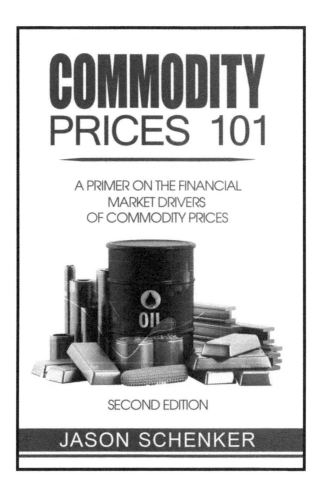

Commodity Prices 101 provides critical commodity market information to help investors, analysts, and executives meet the challenges posed by volatile commodity markets and prices. The second edition of Commodity Prices 101 will be released in November 2016. The first edition has been a #1 Best Seller.

JOBS FOR ROBOTS

Jobs For Robots provides an in-depth look at the future of automation in the U.S. economy. Job creation in coming years will be extremely strong for the kind of workers that do not require payroll taxes, Obamacare, or vacation: robots. Jobs For Robots will be published in February 2017.

THE VALUATION ONION

The Valuation Onion focuses on business valuations across industries, and how discrepancies in valuations often lead to recessions in certain industries, regions, and entire economies. The Valuation Onion will be published by Prestige Professional Publishing in August 2017.

DISCLAIMER

FROM THE AUTHOR

The following disclaimer applies to any content in this book:

This book is commentary intended for general information use only and is not investment advice. Jason Schenker does not make recommendations on any specific or general investments, investment types, asset classes, non-regulated markets (e.g. FX, commodities), specific equities, bonds, or other investment vehicles. Jason Schenker does not guarantee the completeness or accuracy of analyses and statements in this book, nor does Jason Schenker assume any liability for any losses that may result from the reliance by any person or entity on this information. Opinions, forecasts, and information are subject to change without notice. This book does not represent a solicitation or offer of financial or advisory services or products, and are market commentary intended and written for general information use only. This book does not constitute investment advice.

DISCLAIMER

FROM THE PUBLISHER

The following disclaimer applies to any content in this book:

This book is commentary intended for general information use only and is not investment advice. Prestige Professional Publishing, LLC does not make recommendations on any specific or general investments, investment types, asset classes, non-regulated markets (e.g. FX, commodities), specific equities, bonds, or other investment vehicles. Prestige Professional Publishing, LLC does not guarantee the completeness or accuracy of analyses and statements in this book, nor does Prestige Professional Publishing, LLC assume any liability for any losses that may result from the reliance by any person or entity on this information. Opinions, forecasts, and information are subject to change without notice. This book does not represent a solicitation or offer of financial or advisory services or products, and are market commentary intended and written for general information use only. This book does not constitute investment advice.

Notes

Notes

Notes

Notes

Notes

Prestige Professional Publishing, LLC

7101 Fig Vine Cove

Austin, Texas 78750

www.prestigeprofessionalpublishing.com

ISBN: **978-0-9849728-3-8** *Paperback*
　　　978-0-9849728-6-9 *Ebook*